T0003079

CHRISTENDOM LOST AND FOUND

Robert McTeigue, S.J.

CHRISTENDOM LOST AND FOUND

*Meditations for a
Post Post-Christian Era*

IGNATIUS PRESS   SAN FRANCISCO

Cover art:
Triumph of Christianity (detail of fresco)
Tommaso Laureti (1530–1602)
Stanze di Raffaelo, Vatican Palace
photo © Scala/Art Resource, New York

Cover design by Enrique J. Aguilar

© 2022 by Ignatius Press, San Francisco
All rights reserved
ISBN 978-1-62164-593-1 (PB)
ISBN 978-1-64229-256-5 (eBook)
Library of Congress Control Number 2022934515
Printed in the United States of America ∞

To the memory of John Senior (1923–1999),
whose diagnosis of and prescriptions for
Christian culture helped to inspire this work.

Sitting, pen in hand, alone in the stillness of the library, with flies droning behind the sunny blinds, I considered what should be the subject of my great Work. Should I complain against the mutability of Fortune, and impugn Fate and the Stars; or should I reprehend the never-satisfied heart of querulous Man drawing elegant contrasts between the unsullied snow of mountains, the serene shining of planets, and our hot, feverish lives and foolish repinings? Or should I confine myself to denouncing like Juvenal or Jeremiah, contemporary vices, crying "Fie!" on the Age with Hamlet, sternly unmasking its hypocrisies, and riddling through and through its too-comfortable Optimisms? Or with Job, should I question the Universe, and puzzle my sad brains about Life—the meaning of Life on this apple-shaped Planet?

— Logan Pearsall Smith
("The Great Work" in *All Trivia*)

The book is a whole, not a mere collection, not what Aristotle calls "a heap" (*soros*), but a unified and organic work: the parts are not merely juxtaposed but affect and comment on one another.

— Thomas Prufer
(*Recapitulations: Essays in Philosophy*)

CONTENTS

Foreword by Joseph Pearce   ix

Preface   xiii

Meditations

    I. A Lament for Christendom?   1

    II. Methods, Monarchs, and Morals   2

    III. Two Pointed Questions   3

    IV. In Our Place and Time   4

    V. Preparing for Christ's Arrival and Return   6

    VI. Christmas Day, 2019   9

    VII. The Decisive Event   11

    VIII. It's Only a Matter of Time   12

    IX. Who Can Rob Christ?   15

    X. Retrieve, Rediscover, Restore, or Reclaim?   16

    XI. Narratives, Propositions, and an Urgent Request   17

    XII. Time, Boredom, Procrastination, and Other Luxuries   23

    XIII. Manners, Worship, and Justice   26

    XIV. Controversies, Optimism, and Pessimism   29

    XV. Crisis—Chastisement or Illumination?   30

    XVI. Sorrows Old and New, Near and Far   32

    XVII. Friends and Dilemmas True and False   34

    XVIII. Finding Hope between Presumption and Despair   36

    XIX. Gratitude, Memory, Hope, Purpose   39

    XX. J. R. R. Tolkien, C. S. Lewis, and the Prophet Isaiah   40

XXI.	An Exciting Time to Be a Believer?	45
XXII.	The Future Is Handmade?	48
XXIII.	Where Do Necessities and Luxuries Come From?	50
XXIV.	The Roots and Fruits of Civility	51
XXV.	The Works of Homes, Churches, and Schools	51
XXVI.	Who Will Lead? Who Will Follow?	52
XXVII.	What Was Noah Thinking?	53
XXVIII.	The Past, Present, and Future of Hope	54
XXIX.	"I'm Dead—Now What? (Christendom Edition)"	60
XXX.	A Jesuit's First Look at the Benedict Option	63
XXXI.	"Flee. Be Silent. Pray Always." Why? How?	69
XXXII.	The Beginning of the End? Or the End of the Beginning?	75
XXXIII.	Merely Human?	76
XXXIV.	Caesar, Court Jesters, and the Churchians	79
XXXV.	"You Can't Turn Back the Clock"	85
XXXVI.	Moving from "Christendom Lost" to "Christendom Found"	88
XXXVII.	Reconnections	91
XXXVIII.	Giving Our Past to Our Future	93
XXXIX.	The First Principle and Foundation	94
XL.	The Dangerous Liaisons of Church and State	101
XLI.	Great Ideas and Big Plans	105
XLII.	Four Strategies	109
XLIII.	Eight Principles	116
XLIV.	The Hardest Question of All	118
Acknowledgments		123

FOREWORD

By Joseph Pearce

There are two essential elements to the art of teaching. We must know what we are talking about, and we must have the ability to communicate what we know. The necessity of these two elements means that there are three types of teachers. There are those who know what they are talking about but are unable to communicate their knowledge to others. These might be good scholars, but they are bad teachers. Then there are those who don't know what they are talking about but can communicate the appearance of knowledge to others. If they don't know that they don't know, they are merely ignorant; if they do know that they don't know, they are charlatans. Finally, there are those who know what they are talking about and can communicate it to others. These are good scholars who are also good teachers. There are, however, those within this final group who are not merely good scholars and teachers but great scholars and teachers. They have great knowledge and a great ability to communicate that knowledge to others. Such teachers demand our respect and command our attention. Cardinal Ratzinger comes to mind, as do C. S. Lewis and Peter Kreeft. And so does—or so should— Father Robert McTeigue.

For those of us who have the privilege of knowing him, Father McTeigue is both the best of friends and the best of company. One reason for this is his ability to speak on almost any topic engagingly and entertainingly. He has what the Irish call the gift of gab, which is not to be confused with blarney. The former is the ability to elucidate eloquently whereas the latter flatters to deceive. The gab grabs our attention and keeps us attentive and even spellbound. Indeed, as Tolkien reminds us, it is "small wonder that *spell* means both a story told, and a formula of power over living men".[1] For those so gifted, to spell a word is to cast a spell. Father McTeigue is so gifted.

As the title and subtitle of his earlier book for Ignatius Press proclaim, Father McTeigue offers "real philosophy for real people", in the knowledge that such philosophy provides "tools for truthful living". He knows that real philosophy is grounded in reality and that real people need to know the truth in order to live truthfully. His philosophy is steeped in the realism of his masters, Aristotle and Aquinas, but also in the philosophical rootedness of what Chesterton called the philosophy of the tree, which is rooted and definite, as opposed to the philosophy of the cloud, which is rootless, formless and lacking definition.[2] This philosophy of the tree springs from the realism of Plato and Aristotle and has its flowering in the fusion of faith and reason that we see in Augustine and Aquinas. Against this is the philosophy of the cloud, the rootlessness and formlessness of relativism, which changes shape all the time, blown around by the winds of fashion and ultimately lacking substance. This formless philosophy was ridiculed in Hamlet's lampooning of the relativist Polonius, likening a cloud to a series of imaginary creatures.

[1] J. R. R. Tolkien, *Tree and Leaf* (London: Harper Collins, 2001), p. 31.
[2] G. K. Chesterton, *Avowals and Denials* (London: Methuen and Company, 1934), pp. 20–21.

Father McTeigue's approach to reason is firmly grounded, and his head is never to be found in the clouds. Keeping with the metaphor, we can say that the clouds of relativism can obscure the light of reality, casting a shadow over our perceptive faculties, but the obscuring of the light by the cloud should not lead us to mistake the cloud for the light itself. As the great philosopher Samwise Gamgee once said, "Above all shadows rides the sun."[3] And as the poet Roy Campbell wrote in his sonnet "To the Sun", the sun itself is but a manifestation of light itself and therefore a *signum* of the Light Himself:

> Oh let your shining orb grow dim,
> Of Christ the mirror and the shield,
> That I may gaze through you to Him,
> See half the miracle revealed.[4]

The foregoing is a way of seeing things that was exemplified by John Senior, one of Father McTeigue's mentors to whom this volume is dedicated. Dr. Senior professed that it was not possible to perceive reality unless we opened our eyes in childlike wonder. The beginning of wisdom is to be found in the simplest of nursery rhymes: "Twinkle, twinkle, little star, how I wonder what you are." It is only when our eyes are open in wonder that we are moved to the contemplation necessary for the dilation of the mind and soul into the fullness of reality. Such an understanding of the mind's perception of reality is inseparable from virtue, specifically the virtue of humility. The fruit of such humility is the sense of gratitude that is the prerequisite for wonder.

---

[3] J. R. R. Tolkien, *The Lord of the Rings* (London: Harper Collins, 2004), p. 909.
[4] Roy Campbell, *Selected Poems*, ed. Joseph Pearce (London: Saint Austin Press, 2001), p. 46.

Pride, the absence of humility, lacks the gratitude necessary for wonder, which is why pride is inseparable from prejudice. Only the humble perceive the real! Father McTeigue has a humble heart, and he sees with wonder-filled eyes. Furthermore, and crucially, he says what he sees with a five-talented and graceful tongue.

I will conclude this curtain-raiser to Father McTeigue's musings with an anecdotal postscript about an American who finds himself lost in the wilds of the west of Ireland. "Excuse me," he enquires of a stranger he meets on the road, "could you tell me the way to Limerick?" The Irishman pauses, no doubt with a mischievous glint in his eye, before making his reply. "If I were you," he says, "I wouldn't start from here." Irrespective of whether such a reply was very helpful to the American lost in Ireland, I would say, with respect to those who find themselves lost in the cosmos, that the present volume by Father Robert McTeigue is a very good place to start.

PREFACE

Would you like to have some fun? Take the quiz described below. You may be surprised by what you discover!

1. TRUE OR FALSE? "Hey hey! Ho! Ho! Western Civ has got to go!"

   HINT: How this question is answered depends a lot upon who answers it. There was a time when many people would have answered with a resounding FALSE! They would have gone on to add that the great majority of what has long been recognized as true, good, beautiful, has in some way been formed or influenced by Western Civilization. More recently, you are likely to find people answering with a resounding TRUE! They would likely go on to add that nearly every ill in human society, including slavery, environmental degradation, colonialism, imperialism, racism, sexism (and many other "-isms", too many to list here) have in some way been formed or influenced by Western Civilization.

   FOR EXTRA CREDIT: Share this question with your family and friends. What did you learn from them? What did you learn about them?

2. WHO MADE FAMOUS THE CHANT, "Hey hey! Ho! Ho! Western Civ has got to go!"?

   HINT: How this question is answered depends a lot upon who answers it. There was a time when many people would have answered this question with a confident dismissal, along these lines: "This could have been chanted only by people who were so ignorant of Western Civilization that they did not realize that their chanting it without legal, social, or physical consequences proves how humane, rational, sober, and tolerant Western Civilization really is." More recently, you are likely to find people answering with a confident assertion along these lines: "This chant was made popular by people who woke up and saw that the only way to turn back the tide of Western Civilization is to speak truth to power, to resist the oppression they experience daily by whatever means necessary."

FOR EXTRA CREDIT: Share this question with your family and friends. What did you learn from them? What did you learn about them?

3. EVALUATE THIS STATEMENT (recently made by atheist philosopher Stefan Molyneux): "Civilization is Western Civilization. Western Civilization is the Catholic Church."

HINT: How this question is answered depends a lot upon who answers it. There was a time when many people would have answered this question with a confident acceptance, along these lines: "Jerusalem, Athens, and Rome are the three legs of Western Civilization. Greek philosophy and Roman law, elevated and completed by Christian faith, are, quite literally, the gifts of God and man for the whole world. Western Civilization is rooted in time and place; its fruits are for everyone and all time." More recently, you are likely to find people answering with a confident dismissal along these lines: "Such exclusionary jingoism and cultural imperialism are the trademarks of Western pride and Christian arrogance. We are now witnessing the world bursting these bonds."

FOR EXTRA CREDIT: Share this question with your family and friends. What did you learn from them? What did you learn about them?

4. TRUE OR FALSE? "Christendom is a very bad thing."

HINT: How this question is answered depends a lot upon who answers it. Those influenced by Catholic scholar Malcolm Muggeridge—a man of learning and prayer—would have answered with a resounding TRUE! Muggeridge has written eloquently and persuasively that history shows that Christendom was a system of culture and civilization that betrayed authentic Christianity on the world stage, contrary to the wishes of Christ. More recently, those influenced by Catholic scholar John Senior—a man of learning and prayer—would have answered with a resounding FALSE! Senior has written eloquently and persuasively that history shows that Christendom was a system of culture and civilization that promoted authentic Christianity on the world stage, in harmony with the wishes of Christ.

FOR EXTRA CREDIT: Share this question with your family and friends. What did you learn from them? What did you learn about them?

If you are of a mind that such questions, and those like them, should be studied, discussed, debated, prayed over, then studied and discussed some more, because these questions are important, even vital, for human identity and fulfillment, then this book is for you. If you allow me to offer a quick summary of why and how this book came to be, I think you will see that the questions treated here should be discussed with those whom you love and respect and with whom you have sympathy as well as with those who are likely to misunderstand you, or disagree with you even if they do understand you, and perhaps even with those who believe they have reason to despise you.

I was an eighteen-year-old college freshman in 1979. Intermittently, I then spent eleven years as a student, earning four degrees along the way. I spent over twenty years in the classroom teaching undergraduate and graduate philosophy and theology at universities and seminaries. Over the course of forty-plus years, I have read many great books (and a lot of bad ones); was taught by a few excellent teachers (and some mediocre ones); conversed with souls both great and small around the world. I have written, lectured, and broadcasted a fair bit about the questions described above and have thought long and hard about them. Now, having said all that, you would be well within your rights to say, "So what?"

That is a good question. Let me answer it both negatively and positively. Here is what I am *not* saying: "I've been in school a long time! Probably a lot longer than you! That means I'm smarter than you and so you should listen to me!" God forbid that I should say anything like that. I have no interest in setting up my own storefront church as part of the growing "Cult of the Expert".

Answering your question positively: "With the help of God's grace, lots of good luck, considerable effort, as well with the help of some mentors and many benefactors, colleagues, and friends, I have been immersed in what has been called 'Western Civilization' or what may more aptly be called 'Christendom'. I have also spent some time in non-Western cultures. I have had the privilege of studying human nature and human history for a few decades now, and over time I've noticed a few things. One in particular grabs my attention. Since the beginning of the French Revolution in 1789, there has been a growing effort in the West to arrange human private and public life in the absence of any reference to Christ. It is not an expression of my personal taste or preferences when I say that the results in the West have been ugly and disappointing. Many would say, for example, that the arts would indicate the bitter fruit that comes from individual and communal living without reference to Christ. I would agree and insist that a stronger argument can and should be made. One need only look at the appalling mound of corpses heaped up throughout the twentieth century to conclude with confidence that *Corruptio optimi pessima*, that is, 'the corruption of the best is the worst.' Consequently, I am writing to help people re-call Christ."

That positive answer to the "So what?" question should be made more specific with an amplification of the subtitle of the book. What is a "Post Post-Christian era?" Since 1789, a great deal of ink and blood have been spilled to demonstrate that we are all better off individually and collectively without Christ. Some 230 years later, that assertion is getting harder and harder to maintain. I can say with confidence that the "post-Christian world" just is not working. Let us stop pretending. In saying that, I am conscious that the astute reader might surmise that I am calling for some return to the "Good Old Days" or some "Golden Era". I will not do that because there was never any such thing. Since the Fall of Adam and Eve in the Garden of Eden, we can have no access to any kind of "Original Innocence". What we *can* do, however, is to learn lessons—both the good and the bad—from what happened before, during, and after 1789. We can go forward with a clearer sense of what has worked, what has not worked, and why knowing the difference is so important.

What about the concept of "Christendom"? Who do I think is right? Muggeridge or Senior? They both are. Muggeridge is right: "Christendom", as he understood it, is the corrupting leaven of both the Pharisees and of Herod that Christ warns against in the Gospel of Mark. As Muggeridge describes it, Christendom joins with the Pharisees to corrupt religious life by trying to "game the system", to manipulate the divine will, and to ensure divine blessing upon human ambition. Again, following Muggeridge, Christendom joins with Herod to corrupt civil life, limiting human success and failure to within the context of human efforts and standards alone. Herod sees Christ either as a rival or as a domesticated mascot and certainly not as divine sovereign. Left unchecked, corrupt Christendom devolves into what some critics have called "the Business of Churchianity" or, as one witty friend called it, "the *Status Quo Ordo*".

How different (and equally correct) is the view of Senior. He sees Christendom, rooted in the West, offering the good fruits of the marriage of nature and grace intended by Christ. On this view, human flourishing is attained only to the degree that it is truly Christian, and human nature is fulfilled only when it enters into Christ's heavenly glory. In this book, I will orbit around both Muggeridge and Senior. We need them both—Muggeridge for the corrective; Senior for the directive.

What inspired the writing of this book? Taking the long view, one might say that I am paying a debt to both ancestry and posterity. I would like to prove to those who have gone before me that I was paying attention when they taught me; likewise, I would like to prove to those who come after me that I made some provision for them. And I would like to prove to God that I tried to make some "glad return" for all that He has given me. (See Psalm 116.)

More recently, I came to discover the writing of John Senior, in particular his *The Death of Christian Culture* (1978) and his *The Restoration of Christian Culture* (1983). The former offered a clear and convincing diagnosis of what has long been ailing Western Civilization, ailments that Senior feared might be fatal. The latter book offered his prescription to restore Western Civilization to health, namely, rediscovering the habit of Saint Benedict's *Ora et labora* (Pray and work) and relearning the language of love from the Blessed Virgin Mary. Both his diagnosis and his prescription need to be communicated again in our time, especially in light of all that has happened since his death in 1999.

Most recently, the trauma and farce of the twenty-first century, perhaps best encapsulated by the notorious year 2020, has moved me to write, and to do so with a sense of urgency. We cannot continue for much longer down the present path. How much more proof do we need that a post-Christian world is both anti-Christ and anti-man? I want us all to stop and ask: "Are we sure we want to keep on doing this? Isn't there a better way?"

A few words about the "how" of this book. One of the reasons my previous book (*Real Philosophy for Real People: Tools for Truthful Living*) took entirely too long to write was that I was hampered by the mistaken notion that I must first hammer out in my mind, to Platonic perfection, each sentence before I put my hands to the keyboard. I very much wanted to avoid that mistake. Toward that end, I decided to follow the example of my late, great mentor, Dr. Paul Weiss. He had a passion and a discipline for writing. He was willing to take the time to wonder, marvel, explore, speculate, discourse, experiment, debate, and revise. Day after day, year after year, he would type five, ten, fifteen, or more pages of the content of his philosophical ruminations. Between 1955 and 1978, he collected this self-directed Socratic dialogue in eleven large volumes entitled *Philosophy in Process*. He kept this record of his thoughts in order to work toward more confident answers to questions, answers that found their way into his many other books. He also wanted these intellectual diaries to be used as conversation starters for those inquirers who would be willing to learn from them and, Weiss earnestly hoped, would eventually progress beyond him.

I have written this book with a similar spirit and method. Weiss often said, "Good teaching should be the sound of an honest man thinking out loud." What I have tried to do here is to think out loud on paper, and to do so in a manner that would keep me from the "paralysis of analysis" that so slowed my previous work. Toward that end, I resolved to get a large journal and a fountain pen and to write by hand, slowly and meditatively. Moreover, I resolved not to look at any of what I had written until I had filled the journal. I used a journal composed of a brand of very thin Japanese paper called Tomoe River. The journal presented itself to me with 400 pages of blank invitation and intimidation. Whenever I wrote, I resolved to write until I had no more to say that day. I drew a line wherever I stopped. When I next returned to the writing, I took up wherever I had left off, without reviewing what I had written previously. I was adamant that I must not fall into the old habit of second-guessing every sentence; I would proofread once the journal was full. I am pleased to say that I kept that promise.

To facilitate a reading of this book that I think is suitable for its format and content, allow me to compare and contrast it with my previous book, *Real Philosophy for*

Real People: Tools for Truthful Living. Think of a spectrum between Aquinas and Augustine. Here one may think of the style of Aquinas as rigorous, architectonic, dialectical, and demonstrative. In contrast, the style of Augustine is more personal, meditative, rhetorical. *Real Philosophy* may be read as existing more on the Aquinas end of the spectrum. I revised and revised and polished and honed and sharpened and re-sharpened (probably to a fault, as some friendly critics and critical friends pointed out). In reading that book, you may be sure that what you hold in your hands represents the very best work I could do on the topics therein at the time that I placed the manuscript in the hands of the publisher. Did I make the mistake of allowing "the best to become the enemy of the good"? Most likely—that is why it took too long to write. Nonetheless, I can say with confidence that at the moment that I let it go out of my hands, it was the very best that I could do at that time. If I ever work on a second edition, I am sure that I will find areas for improvement.

This work may be read as existing on the spectrum closer to Augustine. One might view Aquinas' *Summa Theologica*, for example, as written with the very fine nib and precision of the architect's pen. Extending the image, then, one might view Augustine's *Confessions* as done with the brush of a watercolor artist. There are broad strokes, blendings, and overlaps suggesting both inspiration and imperfect control, resulting in a work best appreciated as a whole—a whole that would be lost if any individual part were viewed in isolation. I ask that *Christendom Lost and Found* be read as one might read a watercolor painting, and not as an architect's blueprint.

Real Philosophy for Real People, even though it sometimes used stories and humor to convey philosophical truths, was written in a mostly sober and refined voice. In contrast, the tone of the present work may appear rough, unpolished, and perhaps, at least at times, even intemperate. Why not bleach those parts out of the picture? Why not sand down the scratches and rough edges? A comparison to sharpening a knife might help. In forging a sturdy knife for rigorous use, one uses a series of stones or files of progressively finer grit. One may begin with a sharpener labeled "coarse" and eventually move to one labeled "very fine". Using sharpeners in this way, you can sharpen a knife to the keenness of a precision instrument. I think that trying to polish, refine, or sharpen this present work would result in de-naturing it. Filing and smoothing and re-editing would not sharpen it but rather whittle it away. It would be lost.

At the risk of mixing metaphors, allow me one more image to illustrate the style of this work, in order to help the reader enter into it with the right spirit and with the right set of expectations. I discussed this work with my friend and colleague Matthew Maloney. He is the engineer and associate producer of the radio program/podcast I host, called "The Catholic Current". He has long experience in recording studios, both as a musician and as a sound engineer. He told me about the wisdom of "the first take".

He said that when musicians are recording a new song in a studio, there might be a temptation to work and rework a song to the point where there is nothing fresh or authentic left about the song. The song, as recorded, sounds more like a project than a performance, more the result of manipulation rather than inspiration. When trying out a new song in a studio, he said, there is nothing quite like "the first take", the first attempt at the song. Accept it as it came to you—or the song will become lost.

What you have in your hands, then, is a "first take". Reading through the manuscript for the first time, I can easily imagine that some readers might find some passages to be unmeasured, awkwardly phrased, or even objectionable. So be it. I can say that I do not believe that I wrote anything with deceptive or malicious intent. My hope is that readers will approach this work as one might read a journal written in time of war or enemy occupation or plague. The imperfections are an essential part of the story.

What you are reading now was first written by me, by hand, from November 2019 to February 2021. After writing it out, I transcribed it, cleaned it up, and sent it to Ignatius Press for copy editing. As a whole, with some typographical exceptions, the book is presented to you as it came to me. It is the work of someone trying to be a good teacher and an honest man, thinking out loud on paper about Western Civilization, about Christendom, and about whether we can learn from past successes and failures in order to build a civilization that is good for man and pleasing to God.

My hope is that this book may become for you an opportunity for reflection, study, rereading, conversation, prayer, and action.

Robert McTeigue, S.J.
February 18, 2021
Feast of Saint Flavian

MEDITATIONS

MEDITATION I: A Lament for Christendom?

In preparing for my interviewing Coulombe, I read his charming book *A Catholic Quest for the Holy Grail*. It was a well-written book, the work of a careful scholar who loves words and his topic and who loves Christ. What I found in that book was not a whimsical account of a lost "Golden Age", a "Camelot" in many senses of that word; nor was I moved by his stirring up a kind of misty-eyed nostalgia. No. He did no such thing.

He wrote of real people in real times and places—genuine times and places of true saints and sinners, that is, of times and places like our own. Even now, people embrace Christ or ignore Christ or renounce Christ or denounce Christ. Even now, as in the times and places that Senior wrote about, devout souls intercede and keep the sky from falling, thereby buying time for reprobates like me to repent, while I try to corral a few more lost sheep into the ark. He wrote of times and places marked by clarity of identity and purpose. Time, the seasons, nature, all of human endeavor—these were steeped in a diversified yet unified Christian culture. In other words, he was speaking of Christendom.

As a fish is fully immersed in water, so was the Christian immersed in Christendom. The lands and peoples beyond Christendom were mission fields—not so much to be conquered as to be won for Christ. Or, better said, to be won over for Christ, Who already is sovereign over all times, peoples, and places. That sense of clarity, identity, unity, and purpose, I am sorry to say, is no more. Hence, I write this lament for Christendom.

MEDITATION II: Methods, Monarchs, and Morals

I have decided to write this more or less "freestyle", simply as it comes to me, without an outline or any concern for scholarly apparatus such as citations, footnotes, etc. My goal is simply to think out loud on paper. And I do not have a specific outcome in mind for this work, save that I write something that is worth the reader's time and attention.

I think that what I am writing here may draw two types of objections.

The first may be described as an indignation at even a hint of praise for Christendom. On this view, we may wish a prompt, firm, and irrevocable farewell to all the connotations of Christendom including (but not limited to): the Papal States, the divine right of kings, colonialism, triumphalism, the papal tiara, Latin, etc., etc. On the other side (admittedly a much smaller side) are those who may deride me for half-measures, for failing to identify the rightful and living heirs of Saint Louis of France or Blessed Karl of Austria, for failing to bring them to their respective and rightful thrones, for failing to offer stentorian denunciations of whatever peeves such folks keep as pets these days, etc.

Nonetheless, I believe that I can mollify some, enrage many, and confuse even more by bewailing the terrible (and made even more terrible by its avoidability) impoverishment stemming from a widespread misapprehension of Christ as our true king. A regrettable mistake was made when the Solemnity of Christ the King was transferred to the end of the liturgical year. That move facilitates the inference that Christ's reign is only eschatological. No! Christ crucified, risen, victorious, and returning is reigning now. All true order is from Him and for Him. All error stems from disharmony with Him. All discontent stems from lack of union with Him.

Why are some human elements within the Church reluctant to say that? And how many members of the Body of Christ have never been taught these basic and practical truths regarding the Kingship of Christ?

All manner of human ingenuity has been applied to the challenges of social order and human happiness. However ingenious, they cannot satisfy, to the degree that they discount (or even underestimate) Christ.

It has been interesting to watch the development of the work of Stefan Molyneux, now a prominent public intellectual on the Internet. When I started watching him several years ago, he described himself as an atheist, and his atheism was not very interesting or challenging to me. Over time, and ably assisted by Dr. Duke Pesta, Molyneux came to this formulation: "Civilization is Western Civilization, and Western Civilization is the Catholic Church."

There was a time when no objection to that formulation could be taken seriously by Catholics.

MEDITATION III: Two Pointed Questions

Have we really been doing so well that we can treat the Holy Order of the Logos as dispensable? Do we really think we are *succeeding* without Christ?

MEDITATION IV: In Our Place and Time

I have such sorrow for the present state of the Church. (Please understand that I write this as a sinner who knows that he must work out his own salvation with "fear and trembling" [Phil 2:12].)

So many members of the Church today do not know what they do not know, and, for the most part, they do not even know what they think they know. They have so little sense of their heritage, their resources, their opportunities, or their high calling.

Would it not be better for us all to know, love, act on, and teach what the Church has always taught? Why is confusion better? How could ignorance be better? Christendom produced glorious art and noble character—is it really impossible, or simply unwise or somehow undesirable, to live that way again?

In raising that question, I have to address the perennial objection: "You can't turn back the clock."

Well, no, of course not. I do not deny that you cannot turn back the clock. I never suggested that one could. What we can and should and must do is learn from our mistakes. We cannot of our own choosing return to some kind of original innocence. Nonetheless, we can and should retrieve what was erroneously jettisoned or carelessly misplaced or disingenuously recalled and recounted.

A case in point: I write this on the fiftieth anniversary of the implementation of the *Novus Ordo Missae*. (Literally, the "New Order of the Mass"; also referred to as "the Mass of Paul VI", "the Missal of 1973", or the *Usus Recentior*.) What might a reasonable man infer from the fact that this date is not marked by widespread, joyous celebrations of that jubilee?

Now, because there were humans involved, it was certainly true that some priests offered the Mass of the *Usus*

Antiquor ("the ancient or prior use"—an umbrella term covering all expressions of the Roman Rite prior to 1965) sloppily, just as there were laity who assisted at Mass indifferently. Yes, of course. But ... those who have carefully surveyed the record of the past fifty years are less likely to treat the treasures of the *Usus Antiquor* indifferently or carelessly. Summarizing what I have heard from many clergy, religious, and laity in the past fifteen years: "When you've been wandering in the desert for years, you're careful not to foul the oasis once you've found it."

Similarly, people who have suffered the loss of Catholic culture and Christendom, people who grew up on the starvation diet of secularism, those who have suffered the subtle and overt forms of brutality inherent in a social order blind and deaf to the Christ of God—all these we can expect will be well disposed to retrieving what was lost, forgotten, hidden, or misrepresented, and then caring for it well. The past fifteen years, by many accounts, have confirmed this expectation.

The modern project was parasitic upon the good order and rationality of Christendom. Now that the host is nearly (or perhaps even actually) dead, the postmodern vultures have swooped in to feed off the corpse.

P.M.R.U. (i.e., "Postmodernism Rightly Understood") would recognize both the failure of Modernism and the admission of defeat that is popular Postmodernism. A sane and healthy retrieval of Christendom would admit from the outset, and without hesitation, that the year 1274 has come and gone, that time did not stop in 1563, and that it did not begin in 1965.[1]

The project that would begin in earnest, if sanity and fidelity prevailed, would be a refreshment of the truth,

---

[1] Respectively, the death of Thomas Aquinas; the close of the Council of Trent; the close of the Second Vatican Council.

goodness, and beauty of Christendom in our own place and time—a time that (for now, at least) includes the Internet, jet travel, and antibiotics. It would include learning how to live lucidly and confidently while admitting that Catholics have enemies—spiritual, secular, and sectarian—who want us compromised, silenced, or dead.

A recaptured, resuscitated Christendom would generate for our place and time the needed saints, scholars, artists, heroes, and nobilities we so desperately need.

The perennial faith clearly and persuasively articulated and attractively lived can liberate us from the prevalent narcissism and nihilism that are so unworthy of us and so displeasing to God.

What shall we do? What is the first step?

"His first coming was to fulfill His plan of love, to teach men by gentle persuasion. This time whether men like it or not they will be the subjects of His kingdom by necessity" (Saint Cyril of Jerusalem, Catechetical Lecture 15).

Advent has begun. During this time, we are meant to recall that Christ comes to us in history, mystery, and glory. If we fail to acknowledge Him in history, we will be less likely to find Him in mystery. If we do not seek and find Him in mystery, we are less likely to prepare for His return in glory.

MEDITATION V: Preparing for Christ's Arrival and Return

It has been a while since I have written. Christmas is just a few days away. So, this is a good time to reflect upon and lament the loss of Christendom. As I write these words, I wonder if a reader of this text (assuming there is ever a reader) will despair, crying out, "Is he just going to complain for hundreds of pages?"

A fair question. But, no, it is not my intention to complain throughout. It is not even my intention to complain today. Instead, I will make some observations and then offer some commentary on what I have observed.

I did some cross-town driving today. The traffic was worse than usual. Then I walked to a grocery store. It seemed more manic than ever. That scene made me think of what I had observed earlier that day—the swirling crowds at Barnes & Noble and the long, slow lines at the post office. In all these places, no one looked happy. What did they think they were doing? And why were they doing it? Did they believe that what they were doing was worth the effort and expense? There was no atmosphere of joy at any of these places. Is this what people preparing to celebrate really look like?

How different the atmosphere is at the monastery! The Sisters do a very great deal of work to prepare the chapel, their home, and themselves for Christmas. At the monastery, it is evident that the Sisters are preparing for the celebration of something wonderful.

If one withdrew the soundtrack of the so-called "Christmas music" blaring during the scenes I observed today, one might get the impression that these people were frantically preparing for some kind of invasion or natural disaster.

Thirty-nine years ago, I happened upon a short story by Kahlil Gibran called "Eventide of the Feast". It altered my understanding of the Christmas season and of what it means to prepare for Christmas. I will not spoil it for anyone who has not read it. Suffice to say that it is a cautionary tale depicting how Christ can get lost in the shuffle, ignored by people who say that they are eagerly preparing for His arrival.

Recently I read another little work that shook me. It is an essay called "A Remaining Christmas" by Hilaire Belloc.

I am going to undertake the premodern task of copying by hand four paragraphs from the essay. Specifically, I will reproduce here the first two paragraphs and the last two paragraphs:

1. The world is changing very fast, and neither exactly for the better or the worse, but for division. Our civilization is splitting more and more into two camps, and what was common to the whole of it is becoming restricted to the Christian, and soon will be restricted to the Catholic half.

2. That is why I have called this article "A Remaining Christmas". People ask themselves how much remains of this observance and of the feast and its customs. Now a concrete instance is more vivid and, in its own way, of more value than a general appreciation. So I will set down here exactly what Christmas still is in a certain house in England, how it is observed, and all the domestic rites accompanying it in their detail and warmth.

3. It is not wonderful that of such a house verse should be written. Many verses have been so written commemorating and praising this house. The last verse written of it I may quote by way of ending:

4. "Stand thou forever
                         among human Houses,
House of the Resurrection,
                         House of Birth;
House of the rooted hearts
                         and long carouses,
Stand, and be famous
                         over all the Earth."

As I reflect on the Belloc piece, my heart is divided. I am inclined to mourn because he seems to be speaking of a long-lost world. At the same time, I am inclined toward self-pity because I am expecting a lonely Christmas, in an unhealthy culture, before starting a new year with considerable uncertainty.

Even so, I insist that God is faithful, that the prophecies have been fulfilled, and that His promises will be kept. This is the here and now that God has asked me to live in. I must make the best of it.

The Christ of God came into this world and took on all of the human condition. He offers to heal and hallow humanity, that is, the human nature of all individual humans, including me. I want to say yes to that.

Yet I am understanding (is that the right word? "seeing"? "feeling"? "apprehending"?) that to say "yes" to Christ means more than I had realized so far. That "yes" entails more than just "following" Him or "imitating" Him. It requires a union with Him that will demand of me a re-living with Him of His own incarnate life, including suffering, dying, and rising.

Today, I was blessed to visit with Father A. We talked about many things, including Divine Providence, theodicy, and the state of the Church and the world. He says that in this difficult time, we are to unite with Christ and join Him in giving birth to Divine Love, as He did at Calvary. It is for the sake of the triumph of this greater good that God permits the present evil.

I will have to ruminate on that.

MEDITATION VI: Christmas Day, 2019

Christmas Day—how can I speak of lamenting for Christendom on Christmas Day? How could that be right?

I believe in a not merely sentimental, social, or commercial sense of Christmas.

There is a sense in which we must insist that there is not simply a Christmas season but, rather, a Christmas fact.

The Word was made flesh and dwells among us and impels us forward to the house of our Heavenly Father, our only true home.

At the Ascension, Christ did not become an absentee landlord. No! He dwells among us in the life of the Church, especially in the sacraments, particularly the Eucharist.

The Christ of God is with us; He is provident, and He is sovereign. For a little while longer, we can flirt with the world if we wish. But soon the veil will fall, and the illusions, beguilements, and façades will melt away like wax in the blaze of the sun.

We must say that Christendom is never-ending, insofar as Christ is never-ending. At the same time, I must insist that Christendom must be mourned, insofar as clergy and laity alike apparently spurn a comprehensive Christian culture and community, opting instead for the compromises and blandishments of the world.

Mark Twain quipped, "Everyone complains about the weather, but no one does anything about it." In that spirit I ask, "What is to be done about it? What is to be done about the present absence of Christendom?"

Rod Dreher has written of the "Benedict Option", i.e., a way of riding the storm out. He speaks of "seceding in place". My melancholia is sympathetic toward such efforts, even as my Jesuit spirituality balks at the notion. (I must speak of that "Jesuitical balking" another day.)

Recently I conducted an interview discussing "the Trappist Option". The guest suggested that fervent prayer, amplified by purity of heart (itself achieved by an ascetical cooperation with grace), is a way of winning the culture war by pushing back the darkness through spiritual means. I am intrigued by such a prospect, even as I am daunted by it.

In my prayer during Advent, and especially during my Christmas Masses, I have been overcome by the wonder of the Christ of God taking on all of the human condition. Why did He do so? It cannot be because we are so lovable. It is only because He is so loving.

I have always urged parents to communicate to their children, both in word and deed: "You are worth my time." And our Heavenly Father says to us: "You are worth my Son."

Domine, non sum dignus ... Lord, I am not worthy.

MEDITATION VII: The Decisive Event

"He makes His passage into mortal life at a time in which the darkness was beginning to fail and the vast expanse of night to fade away before the exceeding brightness of the light. For the death of sin had brought an end of wickedness that from henceforth tends to nothing by reason of the presence of the true light that has illuminated the whole world" (Saint Gregory of Nyssa).

I have been reflecting on that passage from Saint Gregory for several days. He makes so clear that the decisive event in the history of creation is the Incarnation of the Christ of God. It determines everything else. It is the measure of all else.

There were times and places wherein people—even the majority of people within a given time and place—knew that. And then strived to act accordingly. But here? Now? Not so much ...

Even among the baptized, there seems to be a willingness (or some form of "non-reluctance") to relativize Christ, to reduce Him to just one option among many.

Of course, that is what a sinner always does, right? A sinning Christian barters away the sovereign Christ in exchange for idols. Can any honest sinner deny that?

Right after Christmas Day, we have the Feast of Saint Stephen, followed by the Feast of Saint John the Evangelist. These two men accepted Christ, accepted His reign, and then lived and died for Love.

The next day is the Feast of the Holy Innocents. On that day, we witness the murderous rage of those who will not accept the sovereignty of Christ.

At His birth, Christ is already a mortal threat to the Kingdom of Sin. One medieval commentator noted: "For when kings' wrath is stirred for fear for their crowns, it is a great and inextinguishable wrath."

To the degree that we are sinners, to that same degree we are like those who "fear for their crowns"—that is, we jealously guard the illusion of our own sovereignty as we withhold the love and obedience that is due to Christ alone.

The loss of innocence is a calamity. And righteousness is restored only at a great cost. When and how shall the process of the recovery of Christendom begin?

MEDITATION VIII: It's Only a Matter of Time

How much time do you spend thinking or worrying about time? There are endless books on time management. You could spend several lifetimes learning about how to manage better the time of your one lifetime.

How much time do you spend evaluating time? What do you count as good time, bad time, wasted time? Perhaps more importantly—how do you evaluate our times? Is this the best of times or the worst of times? Are we about to start World War III? Perhaps World War IV? Or are we about to enter a new age of progress?

How much time do you spend evaluating the time of the Church? Are we in a New Springtime, or a Catholic Moment, or are we in the worst time of crisis since ... ?

Before discussing a Catholic way of understanding time, let us be clear: Since the Fall of Adam and Eve, there has never been a truly Golden Era, no truly "Good Old Days". We are fallen men living in a fallen world. Sin has darkened our intellects and weakened our wills. Yet I must insist that God is sovereign over all of history and eternity.

For faithful Catholics, what may be a distinguishing mark of our time is the common habit of seeing time in an un-Catholic way. I would formulate the problem this way: "We are living in a pastless present; consequently, we face a hopeless future." What is the essence of that error, and how can we overcome it?

By a pastless present, I mean this: Many heirs of Catholic heritage have little or no sense of that heritage—a heritage that saints, heroes, and martyrs offered their lives to generate and pass on. We might rightly mourn the common ignorance of Catholic arts, history, culture, etc. We should mourn even more the ignorance of God's Providence, Fidelity, Mercy, and Justice that our cultural ignorance entails. When a "celebration" of Christmas is more about consumption than about worship of the Word-made-Flesh, when it is more about gorging ourselves rather than prostrating ourselves before Emmanuel (God-with-us), then we have proof that our cultural and theological amnesia—that is, our pastless present—must lead to a hopeless future.

Let us look at the West, which has lived in relative peace and unparalleled prosperity since the end of World War II, some seventy-five years ago. One might think that such people would see themselves as singularly blessed and would want to hand on those blessings (as well as knowledge and love of the source of those blessings) to their posterity. Instead, the West finds itself facing a "birth dearth", a "demographic winter", the result of a birth rate far below mere replacement level.

Not seeing themselves as blessed, the devotees of the culture of consumption see themselves with nothing and no one to give to the future. These are the people who do not echo the words of the Psalmist: "What shall I render to the LORD for all his bounty to me?" (Ps 116:12). For such people, heedless both of God and the Church founded by the Christ of God, there is literally nothing and no one to look forward to. Living in a pastless present, they can only see a hopeless future—and then act accordingly.

What is the Catholic alternative to passing through time so mindlessly and heartlessly, living a life without gratitude or hope? Let us "baptize" this philosophical observation from Dr. Rein Staal of William Jewell College: "Tradition anchors our experience of time in memory, and projects it into the future through hope." In other words, there is a thread that links us in the present to past and future. Without that thread, each moment is just a series of unrelated "nows", leading us eventually to crying out in desperation: "Now what?"

We can begin by establishing the habit of rummaging through our day looking for fingerprints of God that we were too busy or distracted to notice at the time of God's contact. We can delve into the history of the Church and see that there are riches of culture and wisdom waiting to be rediscovered. And we must immerse ourselves in Sacred Scripture, so that we see that God never fails to be faithful.

Overcoming our amnesia will enable us to see who we are and whose we are. Such people can recognize as true for us this divine promise: "For I know the plans I have for you, says the LORD, plans for welfare and not for evil, to give you a future and a hope. Then you will call upon me and come and pray to me, and I will hear you" (Jer 29:11–12). With our past secured, we can live with confidence in the present, with hope for the future.

MEDITATION IX: Who Can Rob Christ?

What is my purpose (or, perhaps better said, "What are my purposes") in writing this work, which I had begun by describing as a "lament for Christendom"? This may be a fitting question for me to ask as a writer since it has been more than a week since I last wrote here. I do not want this to be hundreds of disjointed pages united only by complaining and despairing. That would be terribly tedious to read, and it would not do anyone any good.

Dr. Paul Weiss said that "good teaching should be the sound of an honest man thinking out loud." I am thinking aloud (albeit on paper) about an important issue, namely, the collapse (if not demise) of Christian culture in the West.

Some cheer the fall of Christendom; some ignore it, and some deny it. Some see the fall and then counsel the building of arks, the formation of oases, or even a retreat to the catacombs. Some advise a stubborn belief in normalcy, in "business-as-usual". Some urge a bold riding forth, charging ahead, trumpets blaring, pennants flaring—a *Reconquista* (a "Reconquering").

And me? I am drawn by Saint Anselm's motto: *Fides quarens intellectum* (Faith in search of understanding). I believe that we are less likely to find good answers if we do not ask the right questions well.

What can we see? What are we obliged to be because we have seen? What can we see more clearly because we are Catholic? We can see, understand, and act well when we are firmly grounded upon revelation, the Fathers, and the Doctors of the Church.

At the risk of appearing to put myself in good company, I urge us to recall Saint Augustine. During his lifetime, Rome was sacked by the Goths. On his deathbed, he saw the Vandals besieging his city of Hippo. He then penned these words: "Non tollit Gothus quod custodit Christus." Literally: "No Goth takes what Christ keeps." More freely: "No Barbarian can steal what is guarded by Christ." Even more freely: "No Barbarian can rob Christ."

I need to remind myself of that wonderful truth as I see collapse, vandalism, decay, and betrayal. I must remind myself to be alert to God's activities even in the dark times and places. Because I am prone to brooding and discouragement, I have to be careful not to infect others with my melancholy.

I am not ready to celebrate (or even plan for) a *Reconquista*. Likewise, I am not ready to head for the hills just yet. I need to pray more, study more, learn more. Along the way, I will read some relevant material that I hope will prompt more and better thought, which in turn will prompt more and better writing.

MEDITATION X: Retrieve, Rediscover, Restore, or Reclaim?

Not long ago, a prominent person said, "Christendom no longer exists! Today we are no longer the only ones who create culture, nor are we in the forefront or the most listened to."

Taken at face value and in isolation, that statement is inadequate. It is only descriptive, not evaluative or prescriptive. It tells us nothing about how we got to the point where "Christendom no longer exists." It tells us nothing about what has been lost along the way. It tells us nothing about the future we face now that we are here.

I am not alone when I insist that Christendom is not simply one culture among many. It is at once a fully human and graced response to Divine Revelation. History has shown that it is perilous not to build on Christendom's foundation.

What to do about the loss of Christendom? And is not speaking of its "loss" different from speaking of its "end" or its inaccessibility?

I am looking for the right word, or, better said, the right formulation. We cannot, as we are frequently reminded, "turn back the clock", and "restoration" is a dirty word in some circles and an impossibility in others. Can we instead speak of "retrieval" or "rediscovery"? I asked that question of a close friend. He replied: "I like both in tandem ... 'retrieval' and 'rediscovery'. You don't want to 'restore'. You want to retrieve so that you can rediscover." I wonder if there is a place in our conversation for the word "reclaim"? I think that there should be.

MEDITATION XI: Narratives, Propositions, and an Urgent Request

It has been too long since I have written here. Where to begin?

Today, I was contacted by friends from different parts of the country—friends separated by great distances geographically, yet each in his own locale suffering from similar nonsense (as they have described it) in their respective parishes. I told them: "The smoke you are smelling is from the Potemkin Village that is on fire. Too bad most people won't recognize it for what it is until there's nothing left to burn."

Said another way, using a turn of phrase I wish were mine—and whose origins, sadly, escape me: "Not only does the Emperor have no clothes, but the Empire has no tailors."

Who is the Emperor? Well, I suppose that the answer you get to the question depends upon whom you ask. Depending upon the identity and priorities of your interlocutor, the "Emperor" might be identified as (in no particular order) the post-Vatican II Church; the American Republic since the time of Obama, or Bush II or Bush I or LBJ or FDR or Woodrow Wilson or the Seventeenth Amendment or the Sixteenth Amendment or the Federal Reserve or the First Central Bank of 1872 or Abraham Lincoln's suspension of *Habeas Corpus*; Marxism since the fall of the Berlin Wall or Tiananmen Square or Khrushchev's revelations about Stalin; Europe since the European Union or the end of World War II or World War I or the Industrial Revolution or the Treaty of Westphalia or the Protestant Reformation or the writings of William of Ockham; or anywhere in the world other than Europe since the advent of colonialism and imperialism ... on and on it goes.

Let me narrow the field of inquiry and focus on Church history. While admitting some degree of caricature for the sake of summary, I can say that over the years I have met many times the advocates of two competing (indeed, mutually exclusive) narratives.

The First Narrative runs like this: "From the time of Pentecost until 1965, everything in the Church was fine until, one day, an evil genius flipped a switch—and then everything was corrupted overnight. Our only hope is to find that switch and flip it back—as can be seen by those with the eyes to see."

The Second Narrative runs like this: "Starting from Pentecost until Emperor Constantine's Edict of Milan in 313, all was well with the Church—after Constantine's conversion and the advent of Christendom, all was in darkness until 1965, when the Holy Spirt flicked a switch, and we've all been living happily ever after—as can be seen by those with the eyes to see."

There is a Third Narrative that comes to mind: "The history of the Church is long, complex, nuanced. Saints and sinners have always been at work in the Church. There was never a 'Golden Age' in the Church, until the Holy Spirit offered us one, 1962–1965. But that Golden Age was nearly strangled in the cradle by misunderstanders of Vatican II and its 'spirit'. The Golden Age arrived in 1978—and continued throughout the pontificate of John Paul II. Since that time, we have been basking in the glow of the New Evangelization—as can be seen by those with the eyes to see."

It occurs to me that there may be a Fourth Narrative, which may be considered a variation of the Second Narrative. It runs like this: "Everything about the Second Narrative is true, except that the good work of the Holy Spirit (1962–1965) was suppressed during the pontificate of John Paul II (1978–2005, also known as 'The Time of the Krakovian Captivity') and the pontificate of Benedict XVI (2005–2013, also known as 'The Interregnum of the Hermeneutic of Continuity'). Since 2013, however, the Holy Spirit is in charge again, and we can only progress from glory to glory, as in fact we are—as can be seen by those with the eyes to see."

Might there not also be a Fifth Narrative? I want to make the case that there is. But first, I want to state for the record both "McTeigue's Axiom" and "McTeigue's Corollary".

McTeigue's Axiom: "Most institutions would rather die than admit that anyone ever made a mistake."

McTeigue's Corollary: "Most people haven't matured past the age of fifteen and are still desperate to be invited to sit at 'The Cool Kids' Table' at the high school cafeteria."

With these in mind, let us try to formulate the Fifth Narrative: "Since the time of the Fall, there has never been a 'Golden Age' in the Church or anywhere else. Yes, there have been better times and worse times, better places and worse places. Throughout the history of the Church, there have been saints and sinners, the penitent and the reprobate. In all times and places, there have been people more or less cooperating with or resisting God's grace. In all times and places there have been people more or less living in harmony or disharmony with the natural moral law."

How do the Axiom and Corollary help us to understand Church history? I mention them in order to forestall any objections to the Fifth Narrative that might urge its rejection because I am (on this view) advocating for "restorationism" or "triumphalism" or "turning back the clock" or rhapsodizing quixotically in a fog of hazy nostalgia about "Good Old Days" that never really existed.

On the contrary, I am calling for none of those things. Instead, I am urging (urgently) consideration of the following propositions:

1. The history of the Church, marked by both sin and grace, is complex.

2. There were times when members of the Church tried to live the concept of Christendom, and those efforts had laudable elements.

3. Forgetting, denying, or rejecting laudable efforts to live Christendom does not serve the Church or humanity well.

4. Recalling, retrieving, rediscovering, reclaiming, reappropriating the best of the Church's heritage would serve the Church and humanity well.

5. The Church has been in a state of unusual distress for at least fifty years.

6. At least some of that distress can be rightly attributed—directly or indirectly—to the Second Vatican Council and its aftermath.

7. A prayerful, fearless, honest, sober, thorough, systematic reckoning with the Second Vatican Council and its aftermath is indispensable.

8. The Church, especially in the West, is in a free fall across many dimensions, including (in no particular order): demographic, financial, moral, spiritual, liturgical, aesthetic.

9. Refusal to consider, discuss, or even countenance no. 8 is blameworthy—even sinful.

10. The attempt to "save the appearances" (i.e., marveling at the finery of the "Emperor's new clothes") by denying no. 8 and insisting on some form of the First, Second, Third, or Fourth Narratives is, at best, intellectually dubious, perhaps blended with various quantities of wishful thinking.

11. Some attempt at revivifying Christendom (in response to God's grace and not merely as a human project) must be undertaken, for the sake of souls and for the greater glory of God.

12. Undertaking no. 11 is, humanly speaking, unlikely, insofar as it runs afoul of McTeigue's Axiom.

13. Undertaking no. 11 is, human speaking, unlikely, insofar as no. 11 will require surrendering the disordered desire alluded to in McTeigue's Corollary.

14. There are many powers—spiritual, secular, sectarian—arrayed against a sincere, honest, sober, and thorough consideration of nos. 1–13.

15. Because of no. 14, individuals, communities, and cultures prepared to consider nos. 1–13 must be prepared to pay a great, even terrible price.

16. Those individuals, communities, and cultures failing to consider nos. 1–15 will pay a great, even terrible price.

17. Given McTeigue's Axiom and Corollary, a persistent refusal to reckon with nos. 1–16 requires a culture of "permanent lie", as summarized by Alexander Solzhenitsyn: "The permanent lie becomes the only safe form of existence, in the same way as betrayal. Every wag of the tongue can be overheard by someone. Therefore, every word, if it does not have to be a direct lie, is nonetheless obliged not to contradict the general, common lie. There exists a collection of ready-made phrases, of labels, a selection of ready-made lies."

18. Although the demands of obeisance to the culture of the permanent lie are constant, the culture of the permanent lie itself cannot endure.

19. Although the culture of the permanent lie cannot endure, it cannot be overthrown by human effort alone.

20. Every Catholic would do well to reflect on the culture of the permanent lie in light of Our Lady's promise of the triumph of her Immaculate Heart.

21. No one does well as a witting or unwitting servant of the culture of the permanent lie.

I began this work as a lament for Christendom. I pray that it will have a happy or at least hopeful ending. I have undertaken the writing of this in order to make a contribution to (or at least a facilitation of) the overthrowing of the culture of the permanent lie by urging an honest and fervent reckoning with nos. 1–21.

MEDITATION XII: Time, Boredom, Procrastination, and Other Luxuries

This evening, I read a brief excerpt from *Tolkien's Lost Chaucer* by John M. Bowers. Bowers discusses Tolkien's— and I struggle for the right word: ambivalence? regret? guilt? shame?—for not being a productive scholar (especially a scholar of Chaucer) while being busy for decades in service of his "fairy stories".

Bowers (as I understand him) maintains that even if Tolkien's contribution to Chaucerian scholarship that had been published in his own lifetime was slender (at least in terms of pages), Tolkien nonetheless propagated Chaucer's spirit via his own *Lord of the Rings*, etc. I am not qualified to evaluate such matters. Rather, I am using Bowers' reflection on Tolkien as a prompt to reflect on the use of time. I turn to this theme to mine it in service of this project of offering meditations about the losing and finding of Christendom.

An abiding feature of Christendom at its best was a lively sense of the ephemeral character of the finite and fallen world. Yes, of course, high infant mortality rates, low life expectancy, and the limitations on medicine and hygiene scarcely comprehensible to us today all contributed to a vivid sense of the uncertainty of life and the certainty of death for much of Christendom's history.

Of course, for most of the members of Christendom, nearly all of the time, life was *hard*. One might suffer from tedium then but not boredom—by which I mean that lack of diligence then would almost certainly lead to freezing, starving, or a sudden and violent death. "Whatever shall we do with all of our leisure time?" was not an urgent question on the lips of many until relatively recently.

Even so, it was a common theme in Christendom that one would have to give an accounting to God of one's stewardship of the gift of one's life and the gifts of one's life. Perhaps this is what Tolkien had in mind (on Bowers' account) as he retired from full-time academic life?

What about in our own time and times? What about us who have been blessed with health and modern medicine and labor-saving devices and safety? What about those of us who for better or worse have time on our hands, or at least time to spare? What about those of us afforded the "luxuries" of boredom and procrastination?

What have we done with our time? What are we doing with our time? What shall we do with our time?

I suppose it would be expected of me at this point to refer to Josef Pieper's *Leisure: The Basis of Culture*. Fair enough. I must add then that I would be remiss if I did not insist that, after reading that book, one must next read his *In Tune with the World: A Theory of Festivity*. Therein he describes the orders of both nature and grace as gift and worship of the Creator as both a joyful privilege and a solemn duty.

Let us expand on that theme from Pieper. I contend that what he says about worship should also be applied to our stewardship of our gift of time and of all our gifts. In other words, being a good steward and giving an account to God of our stewardship are, like worship, both a joyful privilege and a solemn duty.

Perhaps the words of the liturgy should often (always?) be on our lips: "What return shall I make to the Lord for all He has given to me? I will take the chalice of salvation, and call upon the name of the Lord. Praising I will call upon the Lord, and I shall be saved from my enemies" (Ps 116, 1962 Latin-English Missal).

What a paradoxical era we live in! We hoard our time even as we spend it as drunkards. We give our time grudgingly, say, to Mass, a Holy Hour, or the Rosary, while effortlessly binge-watching reruns of vacuous television programs. (I admit my own guilt even as I write these words.)

Perhaps as we get older, the passage of time weighs upon us more. My father said frequently that, "Youth is wasted on the young." (Was he quoting Mark Twain?)

In the past, approaching milestone birthdays (e.g., twenty, thirty, forty, etc.) prompted me to pause and reflect. The prospect of turning fifty weighed heavily upon me. At fifty, I reasoned that it is very likely that more of my life on this earth was behind me than ahead of me. I am acutely aware that I have been super-abundantly blessed. And I know that Our Lord said, "Every one to whom much is given, of him will much be required" (Lk 12:48). That weighs upon me very heavily. I am not at all impressed (much less satisfied) with the return I have made to God so far. The biblical admonition of "unworthy servants" is my constant companion (Lk 17:10).

In 1983, I witnessed the fatal accident of my best friend, when we were both twenty-one and scheduled to graduate from college in just a few weeks. I have had thirty-seven years since then that he never had. What do I have to show for them? What have I done with the time and gifts of those thirty-seven years?

At my age, I like to quip, "I'm running out of fifties!" What will my thoughts be should I live to age sixty?

I recall reading that at the end of his days Saint John Vianney wept bitter tears for having lived so poorly his high calling as a priest. Saint John Vianney! I can only respond, "God, be merciful to me a sinner!" (Lk 18:13).

What if we believed that at the end of our days we would have to give an account of all of our days? What if we prioritized our individual lives, our families, our communities, our culture on the certainty that it is our joyful privilege and solemn duty to make a glad return to the Lord for all that He has done for us? If we so lived, might not our public and private life begin to bear a family resemblance to the Christendom of old?

MEDITATION XIII: Manners, Worship, and Justice

Recently, I read an essay by Roger Scruton entitled "Real Men Have Manners". Of course, it was well written, witty, and thought provoking. After all, it was written by Roger Scruton. So much of it is quotable. I will try to restrain myself.

Scruton speaks of boorishness as a species of selfishness. He illustrates this with a discussion of table manners. Then he shifts his focus to sexual relations, writing:

> Even in these days of hasty seductions and brief affairs, sexual partners have a choice between fully human and merely animal relations. The pornography industry is constantly pushing us toward the second option. But culture,

morality, and what is left of piety aim at the first. Their most important weapon in this battle is tenderness. Tender feelings do not exist outside a social context. Tenderness grows out of care and courtesy, out of graceful gestures, and out of a quiet, attentive concern. It is something you learn, and politeness is a way of teaching it.

I was drawn to these words: "... and what is left of piety". Why would he say that? I fear that the reason is so familiar that it might not be obvious.

In recent years (decades, really) our general culture has lost nearly all awareness of propriety, ceremony, or decorum. For the most part, we have lost what was once called "a sense of occasion". Illustrations: wearing flip-flops under academic regalia at one's university graduation, cavorting at a war memorial, etc.

Upon reading this passage by Scruton, I could not help but think of the loss of piety and reverence during worship, especially at Mass. I will not review here my oft-repeated complaints against banal preaching, insipid music, ugly churches, tacky vestments, a way of worshipping that one theologian (if memory serves) described as, "casual, chatty, happy, and amused".

How many times have we read or heard (or spoken) these words: "The Eucharist is the source and summit of our lives!" My response to that claim now is, "Why would anyone believe our claim?" Surely, the smelly, sweat-stained polyester vestments and the ill-chosen and worse-kept sacred vessels I have seen in far too many sacristies suggest that the Eucharist is not the source and summit of our lives.

As I am writing this, I have received the following text message from a friend: "Why do I have to remind people to consume the Blessed Sacrament as soon as It is put in their hands?" Source and summit, indeed!

Now I think back to a brief, lovely event I witnessed two or three years ago. It was after Mass, and I was greeting people as they entered the parish center for coffee and cake. A little girl (probably no more than ten) walked by. In one hand, she had her missal and her carefully folded chapel veil. The veil slipped out of her hand and landed on the ground.

Without any hesitation, she carefully picked up her veil. I expected that. It is what she did next that took me by surprise. Without a hint of awkwardness or self-consciousness, she reverently brought the veil to her lips. Then she placed it carefully atop her missal and ran off to catch up with her friends. I wanted to congratulate her parents! In that brief moment, that child showed that her parents had fostered in her habits that would serve her well in time and eternity.

In many Catholic (and secular) circles, a favorite word is "justice". It is spoken of in a bewildering variety of forms and contexts: social justice, environmental justice, climate justice, reproductive justice, etc.

Unlike times past, we do not hear these days of justice and our relationship with God. Why not? Let us ask that question in light of the classical definition of justice: "To give to each his due". What do we owe to God? What is His due? Christendom knew that however one answered that question, the answer had to include worship.

The word "worship" comes from the Old English *weorthscipe* (worthiness, acknowledgment of worth). If we owe God worship as a matter of justice (and, yes, of course, as a matter of love), then the claim that "the Eucharist is the source and summit of our lives!" becomes something even more—the Eucharist is the mandate and measure of our lives! It is our happy privilege and our solemn obligation.

During the flourishing of Christendom, this recognition became the impetus for the cultivation and transmission of such virtues as reverence, piety, decorum, generosity, munificence, magnificence, magnanimity, generosity. These virtues were given concrete expression through the arts and through the custody and diligence of the sacred rites. Christendom was enriched by their presence; we are impoverished by their absence.

How much progress we could make if only we would admit this truth!

MEDITATION XIV: Controversies, Optimism, and Pessimism

I am writing this now in a time of particularly intense conflict within the life of the Church. One of the controverted issues right now is whether there are at present, grave, perhaps even uniquely grave challenges confronting the Church.

In light of recent events, some say that we should breathe a collective sigh of relief while heaping scorn upon the putative doomsayers: "See! Nothing has changed. No teachings have been changed. No disciplines have been altered. All the doors that should be kept closed have remained closed. All that fuss and worry for nothing!" People inclined to be more cautious may say, "We can celebrate because at least we have a reprieve."

My view is different. All the pieces are still in play. There is no obvious impediment in place to stop thoughtful, prayerful people's worst fears from being realized. And while we are all arguing about the timing and substance of changes that may or may not happen, to what important matters are we not attending?

MEDITATION XV: Crisis—Chastisement or Illumination?

It has been a long time since I last wrote here. How long? A couple of months? Three months? Why the delay in a writing project that I say is so important to me?

Part of the difficulty was that I was caught up in the process of relocating. Part of the difficulty was that I was overwhelmed by work demands. But now, here I am, in a quiet and peaceful setting, in a location that is very dear to me.

Perhaps the main reason it has been so long since I last took pen in hand for this project is that we are living in a panic-pandemic. The times are thick with confusion and fear. Perhaps the virus of fear has caused more harm than the flu virus that has set everything upside down.

People have asked me if I think that this crisis is a divine chastisement. I do not think so, because we deserve so much worse. Instead, I see this crisis as a warning—akin to the smoke detector chirping to remind us that it is time to change the battery.

Even more so, I think that this time of crisis is a time of illumination. As Simeon said to Our Lady at the Temple: "A sword will pierce through your own soul ..., that thoughts out of many hearts may be revealed" (Lk 2:35).

I dare not presume to read hearts—that is a divine prerogative. Nonetheless, I can and should say that I do not like most of the words I have heard these days. Likewise, I do not like most of the actions I have seen lately. Where to begin? It is late, and I start tomorrow early, so for now I will only summarize.

I note that we are at approximately day seventy-five of what was billed as a fifteen-day lockdown. We were told to "shelter-in-place" for fifteen days so that our health care providers and hospitals would not be overwhelmed with virus patients. Since then, the goalposts have been moved repeatedly, and there seems to be no end in sight.

The world's economy has nearly frozen in place. The human cost of the economic freeze will be incalculable.

What shocks and pains and scandalizes me the most is that we have had almost no public worship—WORLDWIDE—since March! Holy Week, Easter→ Gone. As if all the parishes and chapels in the world are under interdict.

A brief list of the ugly, maddening, or saddening things I have heard or seen since the quarantine, in no particular order:

1. The Cult of the Expert.
2. Bureaucrats becoming media celebrities.
3. Politicians and bureaucrats ruling by decree.
4. Politicians jockeying for position, using fear and propaganda to gain advantage and to secure even more overt and covert powers.
5. Media pandering to power, promoting fear, acting deceptively, outright lying—even more than usual!
6. A horrifying disinclination to defend the rights of God.
7. Accounts of so many flocks feeling abandoned by shepherds.
8. The bizarre, flippant, and scandalous proposals regarding worship (especially pertaining to the Holy Eucharist) proffered by both civil and ecclesial figures.
9. The erosion of civil liberties and the expansion of State power.
10. The cavalier attitude toward the economic harm caused by policy makers using insufficient data and flawed models, along with a refusal to admit

mistakes, thereby rendering themselves unable to learn from mistakes.

I could go on and on about this drama, but at the moment, it is being overshadowed by an emerging tragedy. Recently, a man died in police custody. The initial evidence looks very bad for the authorities. The full autopsy is not yet available. Much of public opinion is convinced that racism is the decisive factor in this case.

Rioting began a few days ago in the city where the man died. The violence has spread. As I write this, there are riots in thirty-one cities. There have been injuries, deaths, destruction of property, looting, fires. And it seems that most of the functionaries who bungled the last crisis are making a mess out of this one, too.

Lord, have mercy!

MEDITATION XVI: Sorrows Old and New, Near and Far

I am so very sad today. I have been sad for weeks and months, but especially today. Even though I am in a safe, comfortable, beautiful place—in the company of like-minded friends—I feel particularly sad.

Perhaps this is so because I am convinced that—barring divine intervention—things are not going to get better. Not in academia. Not in our culture. Not in civil society. And not in the Church as most people experience her.

In this context, by the word "Church" I do not mean the indefectible Bride of Christ. Instead, I have in mind its contemporary human, institutional structures. These constitute what one commentator called "the Business of Churchianity". It is what Muggeridge called, with disapproval, "Christendom", and it is what Senior would say is the betrayal of true Christendom. In terms of demographics, finances, and integrity, the Business of Churchianity is doomed, throughout this country and the West.

Between the scandals, the financial mismanagement, and the near complete surrender to the zeitgeist, the Business of Churchianity has precipitated derision and demise. The Business of Churchianity has positioned itself between the pincers of irrelevance and persecution.

The managers of the Business of Churchianity, charged with defending the honor of the Virgin Bride of Christ, appear to lack the wisdom, will, and words to do so. That fact is one reason for my great sorrow.

Another reason for my sorrow is the recognition of the irremediable hollowing out of academia in general and higher education in particular. It so pains me to say that! I have spent nearly all my adult life in higher education, either as a student or as a professor. I think that the place and mission of a true (that is, truly Catholic) university are sacred. Not unlike the Business of Churchianity, "Mere Academia" (to make an adaptation from C. S. Lewis) has become a business—no, it has become an industry. It is, in so many places, but a pale caricature of its properly humanizing and divinizing mission. I weep for the legacies of the great scholars, teachers, and benefactors betrayed. Likewise, I weep for the young souls misinformed, malformed, and deformed by these institutions.

At the same time, I am saddened by the loss of civility in civil society. And I must say that the locus of corruption surprises me the least. Prior to my entering religious life, in my few years spent at just the peripheries of power, influence, and largesse, over thirty-five years later, I retract nothing of my suspicion and revulsion in response to that form of life. Even as a teen, I could see that sanity and civility were leaking out of civil society. Nowadays, it seems that sanity and civility are being banished from civil society. Unchecked, there can be only one result—mob rule.

I have to say it! This is what happens when Christ is not known and loved! This is what happens when the social reign of Christ the King is neglected, rejected, and finally forgotten.

Fallen man, relying solely on his own efforts, must fall short of justice. Consequently, he must include mercy and charity in all his relations. But this he cannot do well or for long apart from the grace of God. Availing himself of God's grace is what fallen man has refused to do for so long that now our institutions of learning and governance, as well as our historically Christian institutions of faith and fellowship, appear to have forgotten that accessing divine wisdom via the orders of nature and grace is even possible.

So ... now what? What should I do? What should we do? (And who is "we" anyway?)

MEDITATION XVII: Friends and Dilemmas True and False

Today I received messages from several friends. These folks are all faithful, intelligent, striving after truth, goodness, and beauty. The oldest seems resigned (and peacefully so) to the vindication of his pessimism, even as he maintains hope in God. He has fought the good fight and is prepared to see the combination of farce and tragedy play out. Although the specifics often come as a surprise, the trends, traitors, buffoons, and victims have emerged along the lines that he and I have been speaking about for years.

Another friend, one I have known for many years, is my age and has children entering adulthood. He reminded me that as young men, over thirty years ago, we would discuss over dinners, well into the night, the state of the world. We wondered then whether our pessimism was justified.

He reminded me that twenty years ago, shortly after 9/11, we agreed that there was ample evidence to indicate that the reasons for our pessimism stated ten years prior were not imaginary. Twenty years later, in our present day, he notes: "So we were never unjustified in our pessimism. We were prescient." Even so, he celebrates today because he heard a brilliant commencement address given at the Classical Christian Academy from which one of his children graduated. He can still acknowledge good when he sees it, even in this present darkness.

Another dear friend of many years, with children in their young teens, wrote me: "My main concern at this point is trying to understand how to educate my kids to survive; and I don't mean, 'Do they know how to start a fire?'"

Today was a full day for receiving correspondence from friends. I received a note from a friend who is much younger than I. His children are still babies. In brief, his questions focused on where the present crisis came from—in terms of a root cause—and what should we do next?

Neither of his two questions can be answered simply. I am much more confident in my ability to answer the former question rather than the latter.

Regarding the latter, he presents a dilemma: "Anyhow, I am just trying to figure out where we stand between signing up to help promote local campaigns to 'create awareness' versus digging and stocking a prayer bunker." On this view, the choices seem to be mutually exclusive. There is, on the one hand, the move to lower our aspirations and expectations and to extend our reach only as far as our grasp allows. (With thanks and apologies to Robert Browning.) On the other hand, there presents itself the plan to "secede-in-place" as outlined in Rod Dreher's *The Benedict Option*. Are these the only options? In other words, has my young friend presented me with a true or false dilemma?

Perhaps a more romantic vision of what to do next can be seen in *The Lord of the Rings*, during the siege of Helm's Deep: "Ride out and meet them." In other words, rather than shelter in place, in the hopes of weathering the storm, and rebuilding from amidst the wreckage, choose to mount a *Reconquista*.

Is now really the time to go on the offensive? (Or, better said, a counteroffensive?) Is now the time, as Alfred Jay Nock wrote in his essay entitled "Isaiah's Job", simply to act with blind trust, proclaiming the God-given message, trusting that the faithful remnant will hear it?

Or is it time, instead, as the spy novels' trope goes, to "hide in plain sight"? Then one can serve clandestinely the recusants, strengthening them so that God can do what He chooses. I do not know.

This is what I am seeing: The fantasy of an indefinite "business-as-usual" is unsustainable. I am seeing, too, that faithful Catholics perceive themselves as having been abandoned by the managers and institutions of the Business of Churchianity. For these Catholics, their account of abandonment includes a frustrated desire, they say, for a Catholic education recognizable to Pope Leo XIII, Pope Saint Pius X, and Jesuit Father Hardon. What will satisfy, or at least reassure, the Catholics in distress?

MEDITATION XVIII: Finding Hope between Presumption and Despair

I do not want this work to be a lengthy catalogue of doomsaying. That would be both tedious and destructive.

This morning, I listened to the delight of a faithful friend who is discovering the works of Josef Pieper. I have been reading and rereading the works of Pieper for almost forty years. His little work on hope has been enduringly influential in the shaping of my worldview and my practice. Pieper shows that truly Christian hope is much more than a cheerful disposition, more than, "Don't worry! I just know that everything will be okay!" Christian hope is more than a this-worldly optimism. Rather, Christian hope is the truly virtuous mean between excess and defect. In this case, the excess is presumption, and the defect is despair.

Presumption is an assurance beyond all evidence, an assurance that leads to a fatal passivity. In other words, no effort need be made because the good outcome is always already inevitable. Likewise, despair fosters a fatal passivity because it is sure beyond all evidence that nothing can alter or affect the always already inevitable negative outcome.

In contrast, Pieper offers a demanding yet liberating view of Christian hope. Hope has intertwined within it both the "already" and the "not-yet". Already, Christ's victory is at work in the world. Not yet has that victory been fully realized. Pieper describes the human condition as that of *homo viator*, that is, "man-the-wayfarer", or, put more simply, the "pilgrim". He also describes the human condition as being *in statu viatoris*, that is, "the state of being-on-the-way".

Where are we coming from? Where are we going? Are we merely meandering between conception and death? What if our origin is in the creating God? What if our destination is Heaven as our only true home? A home where already a banquet is prepared for us. What then?

I seem to recall some contemporary commentators on the theodicy of Saint Irenaeus, contrasting his treatment of the problem of evil with the writings of Saint Augustine. In brief, Saint Augustine's orientation was retrospective, looking backward in order to assign blame. (I.e., "Do not blame God—blame Adam and Eve!") Saint Irenaeus' treatment of evil was prospective, asking the question, "What is evil for?" On this view, he is asking, "How can evil be redeemed?" He is also asking, perhaps especially, "How can evil be redemptive?" In this context, he brings to mind the *felix culpa* of Saint Augustine—the "happy fault"— extolled in the Exsultet chanted at the Easter Vigil: "O truly necessary sin of Adam, ... O happy fault that earned so great, so glorious a Redeemer!"

The commentators I have in mind (as I recall them) called this approach "The Vale of Soul-Making", reminiscent of the line from the *Salve Regina* that speaks of us "poor, banished children of Eve, ... mourning and weeping in this vale of tears". They say that Saint Irenaeus, in his theodicy, capitalizes on the distinction between being made in the image of God and being made in the likeness of God. Our progress in moving from divine image (rational, free, moral) to divine likeness (holy) is made only by passing through the "vale of soul-making".

One is made in the image of God inasmuch as one is created as rational and free and, therefore, has moral agency, as does God. One is called to grow into the likeness of God by being purified by trial, overcoming temptation, sacrificing for the sake of love, etc. Over time, taking advantage of these trials, a devout soul grows in likeness of God to the degree that self-seeking has been subtracted, with only love as the remainder. Thus, evil can be redemptive to the degree that one resists it and overcomes it—with God's grace, of course.

What does this have to do with our present hailstorm of crises? These are frightening and dangerous times, without a doubt. But these times can offer us so much more than occasions for experiencing fright in the face of danger.

These times can also afford us, if we let them, opportunities for extraordinary virtue and sanctity. We can discover in these times, if we dare, whether we as Catholics have a good reason to live and a good reason to die.

Of course, I must admit that as I write this, I am (physically) comfortable and (physically) safe, even though I am not at peace. Yet, if I have read Pieper rightly, it could be said that I hope. I do not often succumb to presumption, but I am frequently, perhaps even constantly, afflicted with temptations to despair or at least to a chronic discouragement.

Even so, I see that there is good that I can and should do, that I have some natural abilities that may be of use in our times, and, most importantly, I am ordained to preach the gospel with authority and to administer the sacraments. Consequently, I cannot be an innocent bystander, and I dread the prospect of being a guilty one.

MEDITATION XIX: Gratitude, Memory, Hope, Purpose

When does sorrow move from being a natural and healthy, truly human and humanizing response to loss to becoming something destructive, or at least paralyzing? The social scientists often urge us to let ourselves "feel our feelings". That is a contemporary restatement of a perennial practice. But is that all that we need to do in response to great sorrow?

I believe that there comes a time when one should push back against the weight of sorrow, and, in so doing, one can become stronger. Sometimes, though, we let ourselves become so tired or distracted that we do not realize that we need to push back. We find then that we can barely get through a day. We are vaguely aware that the life is being pressed out of us.

These days, so much is pressing down upon us. And we seem to have so few allies or resources. Structures we had taken for granted—social, civil, ecclesial—seem to be hollow. Bonds of charity, the rule of law, the securities of oaths, all these seem to have been overcome by expediency, fear, or amnesia. It seems that for many, what they have in common with their fellow man is their anxiety, their anger, and their mistrust.

Gratitude, memory, hope, purpose—we seem to be lacking in these. Yet faithful Christians must insist that God is always in act. God is always sovereign. God cannot be overcome. Oh, sinners try to defy Him, but they can do so only for a little while.

God always provides what is necessary for salvation. If we truly, firmly, stubbornly believed what He has revealed of Himself, how might we respond differently to these present trials?

MEDITATION XX: J. R. R. Tolkien, C. S. Lewis, and the Prophet Isaiah

Lately, I have been thinking and reading a fair bit about Tolkien and C. S. Lewis. Both were men of extraordinary erudition and faith. Both were devoted and productive stewards of their very great gifts. Both endured the horrors of the First World War. As a result, both suffered, but neither despaired.

If they were alive now, during our strange and disturbing times, what would they think? How and why would they pray? How and why would they worship? How would they cope with their anger and grief? (I am referring to the anger and grief that were stirred up in their own times and the anger and grief that I expect would be stirred up in them by *our* times.) How would they advise family and friends? How would they advise clergy and religious? What would they expect from the clergy and religious of our times?

Since Pentecost, we have been living in "the Last Days", "the End Times", "the Final Age". Since the descent of the Holy Spirit, "the form of this world is passing away" (1 Cor 7:31). As the reign of God ascends and the tyranny of Satan recedes, we must expect a bitter, spiteful rearguard action from that fallen angel whom Saint Ignatius Loyola named "the enemy of our human nature". The false Christendom is collapsing; the post-Christian world celebrated by the French Revolution and approved by Marxism must and will crumble. I believe we are witnessing its collapse in our times. We must sober up, even as the process of dissolution seems to be accelerating. Yes, "the work of human hands" must tend toward decay—everything that can end will end. Yet the work of God is always tending toward consummation.

Having said that, I hasten to add that I am no way endorsing any form of quietism, fatalism, or despair—all of which are forms of presumption in one way or another. Rather, the recognition of the divinely implanted *entelechia* (that is, the contained-within impetus toward fulfillment) should stir in us a desire for magnanimity. That is, we should be willing to be stretched for greater glory. We should want to contribute to, share in, and reflect the *doxa*—the "shining-forth" that is the glory of God.

There was never a time when an honest Christian could avoid the Cross. For the past seventy-five years, however, it seems to many that it has become easier and easier for larger and larger numbers of people, especially in the West (or, perhaps better said, "erstwhile Christendom") to become more and more comfortable with and finally even demanding a crossless Christ. Christians were warned against this untrue Christ many years ago. Consider this taunt/parody from H. Richard Niebuhr: "A God without wrath brought men without sin into a Kingdom without judgment through the ministrations of a Christ without a Cross."

And this scolding summary from Archbishop Fulton J. Sheen:

> The modern world, which denies personal guilt and admits only social crimes, which has no place for personal repentance but only public reforms, has divorced Christ from His Cross; the Bridegroom and Bride have been pulled apart. What God hath joined together, men have torn asunder. As a result, to the left is the Cross; to the right is Christ. Each has awaited new partners who will pick them up in a kind of second and adulterous union. Communism comes along and picks up the meaningless Cross; Western post-Christian civilization chooses the unscarred Christ.[1]

Granted that we have in recent memory been living in a civilization that enabled a Christian discipleship which found it feasible to speak of Christ without His Cross. I believe that era is rapidly drawing to a close.

More and more, I believe, comfortable Christians will have to decide, quite consciously and quite deliberately, whether or not the kingdom of God is the "one pearl of great value" (Mt 13:45–46). More and more, and sooner rather than later, Christians must be ready to face Christ and say, "Forsaking all others …".

---

[1] Fulton J. Sheen, *Life of Christ* (New York: Image Books/Doubleday, 1958), pp. xxiv–xxv.

What will precipitate that need for such a declaration in public? What will facilitate it? And what will sustain it? We are rapidly emerging into a context wherein the lukewarm will not be able to remain as public Christians.

I recall that when I was a new priest, I would often ask students about their "religious affiliation". Frequently, I received the answer, "Catholic—I guess." For a long time, that vague Catholic garb draped about a practical atheism and indifferent agnosticism could suffice. The distractions and comforts of worldliness could (at least in the "First World") shield one from the discomfort of hard questions and the pain of existential crisis. But not for much longer!

Soon, the crucified Christ will appear too costly or too implausible to very many. And I believe that soon, to a precious few, a faithful remnant, will take up (perhaps for the first time) the ancient cry: *Ave Crux Spes Unica!* ("Hail to the Cross, our only hope!")

Right now, two thoughts come to mind. The first has to do with what has been called "moralistic therapeutic deism". This is a formless kind of theology, most likely to be espoused, I should think, by those who are inclined to say, "I'm not religious, but I am spiritual." This quasi-theology offers a hazy, cheerful, comforting, and comfortable God. This God's highest "aspirations" for us (because the word "commandments" just will not do) is that we be nice and, above all else, that we be "happy", with the proviso that "happy" in this context means "feeling good about ourselves".

I believe that we are accelerating into a context that will preclude very many from feeling very good for very long. Only devotion to and union with Christ our crucified, risen, reigning, and returning King will sustain us through what is coming.

The other of the two thoughts that came to mind as I was writing this was the essay "Isaiah's Job" by Alfred Jay Nock. In short, Nock urges us to avoid the grandiose—applying that word to people and plans. Instead, we should follow the good example of the prophet Isaiah. He received a divine mission to scatter seed, to speak a sustaining word that can be received by a faithful remnant.

That makes sense to me. That is a most hopeful choice. Hope includes a decision to show up, to make oneself available for a possible good future. It is a great form of charity to act in such a way as to facilitate the hope of others. Sometimes we have to show up and remind people that the good has not become impossible. People need to have some sense that they are provided for, not abandoned, not forgotten—not by their neighbor, and especially not by God.

The members of the faithful remnant suffer. They undergo loneliness, scorn, even persecution. When the prophet Isaiah obediently delivers his divinely mandated message, he reminds the remnant that God is at work and that they are not fools for keeping faith.

What would the work of Isaiah look like in our present chaotic context? He would have to speak of death and of the falling away of this passing world. He would lament, weep, and burn with indignation for God's honor when he saw how careless and ungrateful we have been. He would have to be stubborn—stubborn on behalf of God's reputation, stubborn on behalf of the wisdom and triumph of love.

Isaiah today, like the faithful householder who brings forth the old and the new (Mt 13:52), must apply timeless truths to our times and places. A lively sense of history, as well as a lively sense of moral imagination, can be among Isaiah's gifts for the faithful remnant in our times.

MEDITATION XXI: An Exciting Time to Be a Believer?

"It's an exciting time to be a believer!" So said a friend during a recent conversation. He is a man whose faith is lived, not infrequently, at great cost and risk. From him, these are not empty words spoken from a place of comfort and safety.

Is it really "an exciting time to be a believer"? Does it not make more sense to say, "It's a discouraging time to be a believer!"? I think our time may be a season of both excitement and discouragement. First, let us look at the excitement of these exciting times.

Why might now be an exciting time to be a believer? Well, if you find yourself with a hankering to be drawn out of your comfort zone, then this is your time.

I must confess that as I wrote that sentence, I shuddered and lowered my head in shame. What if just one of the innumerable Christians around the world living in fear for their lives at this moment read the paragraph above? Might he not cry out, "Comfort zone?!? Where? When?" and then toss the book aside. I would not blame him. Perhaps I am speaking of, as the saying goes, "First World problems"?

Perhaps one of the reasons that we may rightly speak of Christendom as having been "lost", at least in the contemporary West, is that so many of the heirs (and therefore the stewards) of Christendom never had to consider whether Christendom was worth striving for, sacrificing for, or defending, much less to consider whether it was worth expanding. Perhaps Christendom in our time has mostly been presented as perpetually maintenance-free, neither demanding nor offering much. Consequently, comfortable, distracted, and sedated Westerners could not be expected to rally for what they do not love. Were they ever taught to love authentic Christendom?

In the culture of a fatally compromised Christendom, Christ is merely a mascot or a prop, and His Church merely a museum or a backdrop for selfies. Now that this form of Christendom is apparently dying or even already dead (but perhaps still warm?), discussions seem to focus on what to do with the corpse. A case in point: some of the preposterous and pathetic proposals to rebuild Paris' fire-damaged Notre Dame Cathedral "in a manner more suitable for our times".

So, perhaps the excitement that some Christians feel nowadays may be compared to the lion that is finally loosed from its cage. At long last, it can run and roar and roam as God created it to do. Perhaps now it is exciting to be a believer because now—maybe more than ever—we will discover what we are and are not capable of. And perhaps it is an exciting time to be a believer because now—maybe for the first time—we will discover what Christ can do in us if we put our trust in Him.

Why might now be called a discouraging time to be a believer? For all the obvious reasons, of course, too many to mention here. Perhaps a less obvious reason that now is a discouraging time to be a believer is that we have begun to suspect, quietly—at least at first, at least for now—that many of us have been living a rather self-satisfied lie of a life for far too long. In other words, apart from a professed creed, we have long been living as practical atheists, agnostics, or, at best, deists. That is, we have been existing on a day-to-day level like those who have no living, personal, providential, holy, loving, wise, and just God to turn to or answer to. And maybe too many of us have been living as a kind of pagan—people who see the divine as a dangerous but useful power in the world. On this view, that power is best placated and pacified. Perhaps, like good pagans, we think that this divine power might be bribed or leveraged by perfunctory ritual offerings and by merely rote prayer. (Prayer understood here as mere prescribed recitation, and not as a lifting of heart and mind to the living God, seeking union.) The discouragement may also come from the realization that we may have to live as either an honest atheist or an honest Christian, for the first time. One way or another, our present times will inexorably strip away the mask from all pretenders.

In light of the above, I think it would be better to say, "What a humbling time to be a Christian!" I hasten to add that humility is rooted in the truth. Humility is a simple statement of the truth, without embellishment or diminishment. So let us start by telling the truth:

1. God is truly and fully holy, just, good, loving, and wise.
2. We are not.
3. We need to become holy, just, good, loving, and wise, so that at the end of our days we can see the face of God and live.
4. With unfathomable generosity, Almighty God chose to save us from ourselves by sending us His Christ.
5. If we cooperate with Christ, then we can receive and become what God intends.
6. Most of the living heirs and stewards of Christendom have not cared well—if at all—for their inheritance.
7. The evidences and consequences of our stagnation are becoming undeniable.

Okay. Now let us move on to a modest statement of speculations. The following is a list, in no particular order, of surmises, inferences, and pious best-guesses:

1. Is it not the case that Divine Providence has placed us in this time? Then what is our obligation to God in this time? We should find out; we should act accordingly; we should help others to do the same.

2. Is not everything—every moment, every event, every action, every inaction, every word, every silence—a harbinger of death and judgment? If we believed that, how would we live? More to the point—if we believed that, how would we live differently from how we have been living so far?

3. Do we really think that we do not need ancestors, community, and posterity to live well as humans and as Christians? What can authentic Christendom offer to us that the secularist cannot? I believe that the heirs of authentic Christendom, individually and communally, have an identity, dignity, and destiny that the pagans could not imagine, that the moderns could not understand, and that the postmoderns could not even articulate. Is it not time to stop being ashamed of Christ and His Gospel?

How can we learn to live, and to live well, in the light of and under the weight of, under the impetus of such truly awe-full knowledge? Would living so be what Glenn Tinder calls "learning to live lucidly through time"?

MEDITATION XXII: The Future Is Handmade?

Today, I watched a video called "The Future Is Handmade", produced by a channel promoting a return to traditional craftsmanship. I found the video to be both inspiring and deeply saddening.

It was inspiring because it showed dedicated people striving to make beautiful things. I so admire the commitment to excellence. There is something transcendent about striving to make something that deserves to stand the test of time, something that can be both proudly and humbly bequeathed to future generations. To make something good, by means of great skill and care, for the sake of love—is this not a way of imitating God? How great of God to share with us some experience of how He delights in creation, how He loves what He has made!

Yet the video also made me sad. I am neither an artist nor a craftsman. So be it. But was it impossible that by now I could have learned how to do or make something well? I just turned fifty-nine years old. Surely, I have more time behind me than ahead of me. Therefore, I think more and more about wasted time—time that I can never reclaim or recover. Will God not hold me accountable for wasted time? I hang my head and tremble ...

Even so, it is useless and worse to be paralyzed by such realizations. Better would be to ask, "What can I do here and now and going forward?" What if families, communities, states, cultures, a civilization, asked such questions? What if all the heirs and stewards of Christendom asked themselves that question?

The video on craftsmanship made me sad for another reason. The video's title is: "The Future Is Handmade." It spoke with confidence not only about the merits of craftsmanship and craftsmen—merits that are beyond dispute, even if they are not always evident in our age that is dominated by technology and mass production. Rather what concerns me is that the folks in the video at least apparently assumed that craftsmanship and craftsmen would, going into the future, have what was needed to exercise craft well, e.g., raw materials, well-made tools, the leisure

and safety to learn and hone and ply one's craft, the freedom to profit from what one has made and brought to
market. People who are fleeing for their lives, who are
foraging for food and water, or who are living without
basic hygiene are unlikely to have the opportunity to make
fine or enduring or delicate things. For example, I doubt
whether one could today make a documentary about
flourishing craftsmen in present-day Yemen, Venezuela,
North Korea, or Zimbabwe.

I think of these things because, as I write this, I know
that there are counties nearby that may be suffering loss
of electricity because of wildfires. As I write this, there
are (and have been, very recently) terrible riots, vandalism,
and looting in Portland, Kenosha, Minneapolis, Chicago,
Rochester ... the list goes on and on. Will there be large
gatherings there of craftsmen this holiday weekend, eager
to share and show the good news that "the future is handmade"? I doubt it.

MEDITATION XXIII: Where Do Necessities and Luxuries Come From?

I am—what?—puzzled, confused, saddened—by the
mania for destruction that I have seen in recent months. I
strongly suspect that people who destroy so impulsively, so
thoughtlessly, so gleefully, do not have much experience
in building up. Where do people think that the necessities
and luxuries of life come from? Raw material, cultivated
material, skill, strength, effort, sacrifice, calculated risk, virtue, delay of gratification—all these are necessary for civility's benefits to be brought to market. The conveniences
and necessities of life do not grow unbidden like weeds
sprouting up in an abandoned field.

MEDITATION XXIV: The Roots and Fruits of Civility

I marvel at the complexity of civilization. Intelligent discourse, the rule of law, the commitment to fair play, the creativity and appreciation of the arts, the discovery and dissemination of knowledge and wisdom—these are both the roots and fruits of civility. How easily are they corrupted! How easily are they destroyed! These treasures must be as carefully guarded as they are strenuously cultivated.

MEDITATION XXV: The Works of Homes, Churches, and Schools

As I observe the irrationality and violence let loose in various cities, I shake my head. Are the mobs and mayhem not unwittingly pointing a finger of accusation (perhaps "indictment" would be a better word) at various institutions that were charged with the stewardship of civilization? Are the mobs on the street and the mobs on social media not evidence of the failures of homes, churches, and schools? And who can seriously deny that there are malign spiritual forces at work in the mayhem of our times? I fear that the spiritual tenor of our times tends toward the soporific rather than the martial. That is, those committed to (or at least invested in) what one friend calls the *Status Quo Ordo* are more inclined toward managing decorously the civilizational decline: "Everything is fine; go back to sleep" seems to be their rallying cry. Not much is made of 1 Peter 5 or Ephesians 6.

Some people do know that something is wrong and have headed for the exits. Some suggest that we should head for the hills or the catacombs (however they define such terms). Others insist that the time is ripe for a *Reconquista*—that is, the approach of "the best defense is a good offense." What would that look like? Who would do it? Who would lead it?

MEDITATION XXVI: Who Will Lead? Who Will Follow?

What is needed in these our times? What resources? Perhaps it is better to ask, "*Who* is needed?" One might be tempted to attempt grand but futile gestures. Or one might ask for the grace of hope, a hope at once stubborn *and* active. I think of this passage from volume 2 of *The Lord of the Rings*:

> "Nonetheless day will bring hope to me," said Aragorn. "Is it not said that no foe has ever taken the Hornburg, if men defended it?"
>
> "So the minstrels say," said Éomer.
>
> "Then let us defend it, and hope!" said Aragorn.

Is the above an apt description of our condition? I think not. At the siege of Helm's Deep, neither the attackers nor the defenders denied that a siege was underway. Not so for our times, I fear.

A few pages later, King Théoden considers a last, desperate gesture—an opportunity to die bloodied but unbowed:

> "It is said that the Hornburg has never fallen to assault," said Théoden; "but now my heart is doubtful. The world changes, and all that once was strong now proves unsure. How shall any tower withstand ... such reckless hate?"

Finally, Théoden decides to act:

> "The end will not be long," said the king. But I will not end here, taken like an old badger in a trap.... When dawn comes, I will bid men sound Helm's horn, and I will ride forth. Will you ride with me then, son of Arathorn? Maybe we shall cleave a road, or make such an end as will be worth a song—if any be left to sing of us hereafter."
>
> "I will ride with you," said Aragorn.

My first thought upon my most recent read of that exchange: "At least Théoden is not alone!" Here, I must pause and check myself. Some perspective is needed. If I look out my window, my eyes do not fall upon scenes of slaughter witnessed by a silent world, the kind of slaughter I would see if I looked out my window as a white farmer in South Africa or as a Christian in Nigeria, or as a Tibetan monk in my own country. Even so, the decay of the West, what was once known as Christendom, stifles those who might otherwise have been able to respond to those genocides. If we are silent or stifled in the face of genocide, how we can speak of working effectively to rebuild a Christian civilization?

MEDITATION XXVII: What Was Noah Thinking?

What if we recognized that our own present situation is beyond human remedy? By "situation", I mean, first of all, the dynamics toward collapse that I see in the United States in respect to civil society, academia, and what I have been calling "the Business of Churchianity". If we want the concept of the "situation" to be more expansive, I would include Western Civilization in general and Western Europe in particular. Regarding all of these, I would say that no amount of human ingenuity, creativity, good will, and honest effort could pull us back fully from the unfolding calamity.

Profound conversion, leading to a brightening of intellect, a correcting and strengthening of will, and a renewal of charity—all these, while necessary for cooperating with divine intervention, certainly cannot replace divine intervention. Too much has been lost, broken, or forgotten. The rot, corruption, and perversion are too deep and wide to be remedied by anything other than an act of God.

I wondered if such thoughts ever occurred to Noah? If so, did they occur before or after God told him to build the ark? Did they come to him while he was building the ark? Or only after he boarded the ark?

MEDITATION XXVIII: The Past, Present, and Future of Hope

So much has happened since I last wrote. I do not know where to start or how to proceed. I am reluctant to go into specific details from headlines and the like, for fear that these may become dated distractions for the reader.

I will say this: I am thinking much, much more about death these days and of the passing qualities of this world. I do this even though I am not quite sixty and, as far as I know, I am in good health. Nonetheless, I think more and more about death and about ordinary features of life fading away or being wrenched away. Our contemporary world is so very complex and interconnected and, therefore, so very fragile.

I watch with sorrow and foreboding the dissolution of three dimensions of public life and am uncertain whether any phoenix will rise from the ashes.

1. The dissolution of civil society: We are on the verge of witnessing a progressively rapid unravelling of what I years ago called, "the conditions of possibility for being together well". We are living through what one author called "the loss of civility". Our ability to cooperate, to agree on what is just, to govern with true legitimacy—I doubt that these will be within our reach again any time soon.

2. The dissolution of the institutional dimension of the Church: what some have called "the Business of Churchianity" or the *Status Quo Ordo*. This is a way of living discipleship that is neither costly nor fruitful. The Business of Churchianity, at least in the West, has been in a demographic and financial death spiral for years. Very recent events have greatly accelerated this process, including civil society insisting (often backed with force) that worship is "nonessential". By many accounts, recent scandals and prolonged fatuities have made pronouncements from prominent Church figures irrelevant or worse.

3. The rotting and collapse of academia: I am told often by brokenhearted alumni that the academy has betrayed its sacred mission. When I see the violence and hear the slogans of university students running amok, when I read the screeds of their professors, I find myself choking on anger, grief, and indignation. What a corruption of souls!

There is a good way to die, is there not? There is a noble and holy way of surrendering the passing things of this world. But ... the kind of "death" I am experiencing now is something different. It is akin to holding a living treasure in your hands, sensing it turning to ashes—because of a lack of love. With horror in the present, as one turns with sorrow toward the impending barren future, the pain is worsened by the jeers of those welcoming the demise of what should have lasted longer.

People speak of schism in the Church. They speak of secession or civil war in politics. They speak of the failure and collapse of institutional education. Who speaks of hope? Who speaks of our debt to our heritage and to our ancestors? Who speaks of our obligation to our posterity and to our future? How shall we invoke God at this time of illumination before the time of trial begins in earnest? How do we prepare our young people for the future? And how shall we explain to them the diminishments we are bequeathing to them?

Enough! I said that I would speak of hope.

Hope, real hope, can only rest upon the foundation of God, who is good, wise, provident, and faithful. He cannot fail. Saint Ignatius Loyola said that the grace necessary for salvation is always available to us. We must not—we dare not—think and feel and speak and act as spiritual orphans.

While there is still time, we need to rediscover and reclaim our Catholic heritage, which can help sustain us during the coming trials. We need to relearn the spiritual and corporal works of mercy. We need to be able to articulate again the necessity and practice of worthy worship.

And somehow—we need to evidence the joy that is proper to a redeemed people. This is a joy that the world cannot give and that the world cannot take away. Was it not Nietzsche who said, "I'd be more inclined to believe in the Christian savior if Christians looked like they were saved"?

Hope requires a special kind of sobriety, a sobriety that chastens the giddiness of presumption and rebukes the resignations of despair.

I have noticed that most people speak of hope in terms of a desired future good that may come to them. That is an important part of hope, but only a part. Hope is also the present conviction that one has something good to give to the future. We may see this rather simply in a man planting a tree, while sure that he will not live long enough to enjoy its shade. We may see this more grandly in the life of a community that begins to build a cathedral, sure that none of its members will live long enough to worship in it.

The first mode of hope, as described above, is rooted in a recognition that one is loved. The second mode of hope, as described above, is rooted in a recognition that one can love. The two are related.

Do ut des. (I give, so that you might give.) What to make of this phrase? Well, Saint Ignatius Loyola said that lover and beloved delight in exchanging gifts. And Saint Bernard of Clairvaux said that we become like what we love. If we can tie these two strands together, we can gain much clarity and insight regarding hope. I should clarify that *Do ut des* is not a strategy; it is not a technique for bribing others to reciprocate. Rather, God says, "I give so that you might give—and thereby know the joy that I find in giving."

God is infinite and self-sufficient. God lacks no good. Consequently, God as creator does not create from any need or lack. God only creates from sheer generosity.

God creates us from nothing. Creation *ex nihilo* is an infinite, absolute act. He can so act because He is the Supreme Being and therefore omnipotent. Lacking no good or perfection, God is generous, wise, provident, and loving.

The hallmark of love is to will the best for the beloved. What does God will for us, His beloved? The best. And the best for us is God Himself. He wishes us to share in His joy of perfect generosity. This we can do (within our human limitations) by becoming like Him in loving with generosity and without self-seeking. Now we can come back to *Do ut des*—I give so that you might give. And we can link this giving to hope.

Consider the first mode of hope that we discussed earlier—the choice to make oneself available to a possible good future. Such a stance makes sense only if one has had an awareness of being the beloved of a benevolent lover—in this case, the Divine Lover.

Grateful for generous love, one becomes eager to be like the Divine Lover, the One who loves without self-seeking. This understanding takes us to the second mode of hope described above—that of choosing to donate to a future that (humanly speaking) one would not be able to enjoy.

Now let us relate all this to the overarching theme of these meditations, which is Christendom. Christendom—that panoply of meaning—Christendom, that rich, rich tapestry of the True, the Good, and the Beautiful—has been entrusted to the Church as a wedding gift from her Bridegroom, who is Christ Himself.

To know Christendom is to delight in a feast of the senses of body and soul. To know Christendom is to know the love of God, a love handed to us by fallen sinners striving to be saints. Anyone with a living soul, upon receiving such love, will desire more. Such a soul will face the future living and praying with open hands.

Likewise, such a delighted beloved will want to imitate the Divine Lover. Such a beloved will cry out, "*Do ut des!*" The beloved will so cry out, first to the Divine

Lover, so as to indicate that the beloved has learned the lesson that the Divine Lover wished to teach.

At the same time, the beloved will cry out to the future, to the not-yet-realized, imitating the Divine Lover by giving without self-seeking. That self-donation is an act of generosity, meant to be fruitful. It is also meant to be an imitation—however pale, incomplete, imperfect—of the initial, infinite gift.

We heirs of Christendom have such a profound obligation! And such a privileged opportunity! We have an obligation to receive well and to know and love the wisdom, arts, and crafts of Christendom. We have an obligation to immerse ourselves in them, to savor them. And in an act of hope, we may choose to make ourselves available to another possible reception in the future, a future reception of a benefaction from Christendom. "For to him who has will more be given, and he will have abundance; but from him who has not, even what he has will be taken away" (Mt 13:12). In other words, an act of hope in the first mode.

Likewise, we must be such good and grateful heirs of Christendom that we will gladly and earnestly strive to become good stewards of Christendom. We must choose to make Christendom available to the future, to those who cannot benefit us, perhaps not even know us. In other words, an act of hope in the second mode.

What if we were to build our individual and communal lives as people of hope, that is, as people in the present, lucidly aware of being between past and future, fully aware that we are heirs who must be benefactors, who are both blessed and blessing? What would our lives look like then? What would be our concerns and priorities then? How would we spend our time, energy, and resources? What would then be worthy of our worship and our leisure?

There are no short and simple answers to these questions. But surely, we could say that if we lived as people of hope, as worthy heirs and stewards of Christendom, then our lives would look and feel very different from what so many of us have been living in recent—what? Months? Years? Decades?

Can any one of us, can any group of us honestly say that we have been living wisely and well our vocation as heirs and stewards of Christendom?

MEDITATION XXIX: "I'm Dead—Now What? (Christendom Edition)"

Not long ago, I stumbled upon a book with an arresting title: *I'm Dead—Now What?* The subtitle removes any doubt about the purpose of the book: *Important Information about My Belongings, Business Affairs and Wishes*. At a price of only $13.49, the book costs less than hiring a lawyer to draw up a will. I can easily imagine the book being bought by someone who is elderly or who just received a terminal medical diagnosis. Using such a book would be an act of charity on behalf of the loved ones you leave behind. If you are an especially orderly person, or an anxious planner, the book makes a lot of sense.

Two thoughts about this book:

1. The book, once filled out, might sit on a shelf gathering dust for years or even decades. What if the timeline were very short? As a priest, I have been on the scene many times where a patient has been described as "actively dying". You expect that person to die in a matter of hours or even minutes. What "arrangements" could be made then? There is little time or

opportunity for planning then—hence the appeal of lawyers and wills, or at least a notebook with plans made with forethought rather than haste.

2. What kind of preparations can and should be made when it is not just an individual facing death? For example, in the West, many women's religious communities have been in steep decline for years, even decades. When the process of decline was finally seen as irreversible, the community members spoke of "the grace of diminishment". Nowadays I have heard of community members speaking of "the grace of completion". Discussing this with one of my more sardonic friends, he quipped, "What comes next? The grace of oblivion?"

Let us expand the frame of reference. What if what you needed to plan for was not the death of an individual or the demise of a community? What if you had to plan for the passing away of a culture? Or a civilization? What if you had to fill up a volume entitled: *I'm Dead—Now What? (Christendom Edition)*.

Here I will pause to allow the expected reflex reactions to play out. "But what about Matthew 16:18? What about Our Lord's promise to Saint Peter that the gates of Hell shall not prevail? What about that?" Whatever that Gospel verse might mean (and I do not think it means what many people think it means), my reading of the text was irrevocably marked by this observation made by Maureen Mullarkey: "We misunderstand the 'gates of hell' trope if we take it as a promise that Saint Peter's will not suffer the fate of the Hagia Sophia."

Let me be clear about what I am *not* saying. I am not saying that the Church will or can disappear. The divinely constituted Church, the Bride of Christ, is imperishable.

What I am speculating about is the collapse, the demise, the effacing of Christendom. And I am using the word "Christendom" in the two senses first discussed at the outset of this book. First, I am speaking in this context of the dissolution and fading of "Christendom" with all its positive connotations, in the manner of John Senior. That is, Christendom as the web of cultures of shared values, beliefs, virtues, and commitments. This is Christendom as the way of sensing, feeling, thinking, relating, and prioritizing that facilitated the flourishing of the arts, the growth of monasteries, the founding of universities, and the building of great cathedrals.

At the same time, by the demise of "Christendom", I am using that word with all of its negative connotations, in the manner of Malcolm Muggeridge. This is Christendom that has been variously described as "the Business of Churchianity", as the *Status Quo Ordo*, as the network of maintenance-level faith communities requiring little and offering even less.

I make bold to suggest here that the demise of Christendom as John Senior understands it, even if inevitable, is to be lamented and, where possible, forestalled and mitigated. At the same time, the demise of Christendom negatively understood, as Malcolm Muggeridge described it, is as inevitable as the demise of Christendom in the first sense (perhaps even more so). Its passing should be humbly accepted, soberly celebrated, and enshrined in memory as a dreadful cautionary tale.

Our task is this: to make hopeful plans regarding the future of Christendom. And I mean hopeful in both modes discussed earlier in this book. We need to be hopeful in the recipient mode, making ourselves available to a possible good future.

Concurrently, we need to speak of hope in the second mode, that is, in the more active and donative sense of the word. We must be good stewards of the treasures of Christendom bequeathed to us, bequeathing them in turn to future generations. The death of weeds and the planting of seeds—that is what is required by the impending passing of Christendom(s).

MEDITATION XXX: A Jesuit's First Look at the Benedict Option

I suppose that it is inevitable that one writing nowadays about Christendom, and post-Christendom (and perhaps even post post-Christendom), will have to speak about the "Benedict Option", especially as it has been popularized by Rod Dreher in his *The Benedict Option: A Strategy for Christians in a Post-Christian Nation*. I have an interesting history with the concept of the Benedict option.

In the summer of 1991, I was wrapping up my first year as a Jesuit novice. The novices were taking a little vacation break at the Jersey Shore. One of the books I had brought with me was *After Virtue* by Alasdair MacIntyre. (I really should read it again, and I understand that there were later editions.) What stood out for me then, and to this day, is the last paragraph of the book, which, if I understand the matter correctly, Dreher took as an inspiration for his own book, *The Benedict Option*.

Here is a quick summary of my recollection of the book I read all those years ago, along with how that recollection has fermented since that time. MacIntyre, in that last paragraph—cautiously—draws parallels between the decline of the Roman Empire and subsequent emergence of a Dark Age and the "new dark ages already upon us", at least in Europe and America. (Remember that the first edition of the book was published in 1981!)

He calls for the construction of local forms of community within which civility and the intellectual and moral life can be sustained. In other words, the reigning paradigm of culture had once collapsed, yet a faithful remnant survived and grew to flourish (into what we are here calling "Christendom" in the best sense of the word). That the civilizational phoenix emerged from the ashes is proof that such a resurrection is not impossible and could happen again, beginning with us in our own time.

MacIntyre notes, however, a distinctive difference between then and now: "This time, however, the barbarians are not waiting beyond the frontiers; they have already been governing us for quite some time. And it is our lack of consciousness of this that constitutes part of our predicament. We are waiting not for a Godot, but for another—doubtless very different—Saint Benedict."

Here is how I would summarize in cursory fashion my understanding of MacIntyre in the summer of 1991: Saint Benedict built monastery walls around communities that prayed and copied manuscripts. Behind the safety of those walls, Saint Benedict and those who came after him kept alive a distinctively Christian way of putting to use human hands, hearts, minds, and voices. When the sounds of the barbarians slaughtering each other eventually did recede, the Benedictines lowered their drawbridges and evangelized those who remained—and so began Christendom.

How did my young Jesuit self respond to that understanding of the Benedict Option? I remember closing the book and saying to myself: "I can't do that—I'm a Jesuit." I reasoned then that it is the vocation of a Jesuit, not to pull up the drawbridges, but rather to live (and likely die, as our martyrology shows) in the thick of things. If I am able and Divine Providence permits, I would like someday to write a more detailed and structured work entitled, "A

Jesuit Looks at the Benedict Option". (Perhaps this present work is a first draft?)

Dreher advises us to "secede spiritually from the mainstream". This would (as I understand him) entail being more intentional, comprehensive, and communal about living, as Scripture says, "in the world but not of the world" (see Jn 17:14–16). It is not really a final call to build the ark or retreat into the catacombs.

One living the Benedict Option might still pay one's bills by toiling in the workaday world, in the venue that I have called elsewhere "the realm of common experience". But the center of gravity for one's life would be elsewhere. Rather than identifying oneself by what one produced and consumed, one would instead focus on worship, community, and simplicity. The domestic "monastery" of the family home would be networked with other similar families, with the manner and degree of affiliation and interaction to be decided locally. This way of living would keep body and soul together and keep alive a Christian heritage and witness that could be handed down to future generations. It would be a way of living that would allow Christian communities to survive and even flourish in a cultural context that has grown indifferent to or even impervious to Christian witness.

But what if Dreher understates or mischaracterizes what is barbarous about the barbarians in this age of the Benedict Option? I have in mind Dr. Anthony Esolen, whose work and character I greatly admire. A few years ago I spoke with him after he gave a lecture based on his book *Out of the Ashes: Rebuilding American Culture*. His tone is sharper than that of Dreher. Esolen derides contemporary theologians (both professional and amateur) who urge Christians to "evangelize the culture". (What that means is never precisely articulated. As far as I can tell, it has something to do with "meeting people where they're at", as if people could be met anywhere else. How can you meet people where they are *not*?) "Evangelize the culture!", Esolen scoffed. "We don't have a culture! We have a sewer! Our first step is to get out of the sewer. Then we can talk about evangelizing the culture."

I think that Esolen is closer to the mark than Dreher. The present cultural context of the West is not simply indifferent to Christianity. It is inimical to and corrosive of Christian faith and morals.

And since the onset of what I have called "The Covid Interruption", we have seen that the "post-Christian West" is becoming more willing to use threats of force and actual violence (both State-sanctioned and otherwise) against Christian individuals and Christian communities. I believe that Christian communities in Nigeria, Iraq, Armenia, and China have a lot to tell us about what we have to look forward to in the West.

What would I say to those who insist that now is the time for a new *Reconquista*—a new, vigorous, and comprehensive pushing aback against the barbarians on all fronts? What do I say to those kindred spirits of the *Reconquistas* who insist that "the best defense is a good offense"?

Let me put it this way: Do you really believe that you and the Christians you know are ready for such a vigorous initiative? Who would call it? Who would lead it? To which banner would worthy stalwarts rally? Unfurling a banner declaring, "We just want to be left alone!" or "Let's get back to normal!" would seem to me to be a fruitless gesture. Of course, something much, much bolder would be called for. But what? Many would-be banners from across the political and theological spectrums come to mind—some satirical, some poignant, all likely to be fruitless. Could sufficient cultural forces even agree on where to begin? We have some hard thinking and rethinking to do.

Let us start by talking to men who have already engaged in real life-and-death struggles. I remember having a conversation with some Marines and a Navy corpsman. I asked them, "How do you render first aid to a wounded comrade?" The Marines agreed, "First aid begins with returning fire with superior firepower."

Then what? The Navy corpsman told me, "You have to get off the X." The "X" is the spot where your comrade was shot and went down. The "X" is within the reach of the enemy. Therefore, it is the spot where any would-be rescuers could be shot. Hence the maxim, "Get off the X."

This advice, as I see it, combines elements of offense and defense. In terms of Christians caught in a cultural crossfire, both Christians and non-Christians alike need to see that Christians are not pushovers. The dynamic of counteroffensive can be seen in Christians living out the demands of 1 Peter 3:15: "Always be prepared to make a defense to any one who calls you to account for the hope that is in you." Such Christians might include apologists, scholars, lawyers, broadcasters, artists, statesmen, as well as parents who proudly put on their van a sticker that reads: "Yes, these ARE all my children!" Going on the offensive in the truest sense of the term, in this context, I take to mean winning over to the banner of Christ both the indifferent and the hostile. But that is another topic for another time ...

Aiding the wounded by "getting off the X" is an urgent task of spiritual first aid. Wounds must be staunched, purified, and secured before they can be healed. And there are tasks that must be seen to before anyone is able to render aid to the wounded.

Prior to equipping teams for the mission of search-and-rescue, there must be a "green zone", a place of safety. For Christians in a hostile cultural environment, the green zone might take the form of a monastery, a parish, a school, or a family home. That place of safety must exist and *must be known to exist*. There the essential bonds of camaraderie, common cause, and common practice can be formed. Likewise, the green zone is the place where the wounded can be brought to recover, with an eye—ideally—toward getting the wounded strong enough to get back on the field again.

If discussion of *Reconquista* or "going on the offensive" or "mounting a cultural counteroffensive" is to move beyond mere talk *and* not end in a fruitless or suicidal gesture, Christian communities will need a variety of teams with a variety of skills. There are those who will manage the green zones wherein both training and recovery can take place. There are those who must be willing to engage in the dangerous and often thankless work of search-and-rescue. There must be those who are willing to go out and win back the lost. And there must be those willing to push back the frontiers of a hostile culture.

Let us go back to the idea of "getting off the X". If the fallen comrade denies that he is wounded, his cooperation with his rescuers is unlikely. If the comrades of the man obviously bleeding out deny that he has been wounded at all, then no effort at rescue will be made. And if most of the people on the field deny that there is any conflict at all, well ...

Let us take these battlefield images and apply them to our analysis of Christendom lost and found, and let us complicate the matter by adding McTeigue's Axiom: "Most institutions would rather die than admit that anyone ever made a mistake." Those described by the Axiom are like those who deny that the bleeding comrade is wounded at all. Now let us add in McTeigue's Corollary: "Most people have not matured past the age of fifteen and are still desperate to be invited to sit at 'the Cool Kids' Table' at the high school cafeteria." Or, perhaps more simply: "Most people are dreadfully desperate for approval." Those described by the Corollary would deny that any conflict is taking place at all. Such conflict-averse people are incapable of participating in any *Reconquista* or Cultural Counteroffensive.

In terms of Christendom lost and found, "getting off the X" would entail at least the following:

1. People who admit that Christendom is gravely, perhaps mortally wounded.
2. People who believe that Christendom is worth rescuing.
3. People who understand that "returning fire with superior firepower" in this context will require people skilled in apologetics, spiritual warfare, and the spiritual and corporal works of mercy.
4. People who understand that there must be a "green zone" from which rescuers can emerge and to which the wounded can be brought. (These can be, but need not be, one and the same place.)

If there are individuals and communities committed to and able to get wounded Christendom "off the X", then, perhaps we can have a serious discussion about a *Reconquista* or cultural counter-offensive.

MEDITATION XXXI: "Flee. Be Silent. Pray Always." Why? How?

Alfred Jay Nock, in his important essay "Isaiah's Job", rightly warns us against those who claim that they have a universal solution. We should be especially on our guard, he says, against those whose purported solution, they say, will surely succeed—on the condition that we give them sufficient power. I am certainly not recommending any one-size-fits-all solution in this present work.

In fact, I do not think the word "solution" applies in this context at all. This is so because we have brought ourselves to a condition that is beyond human remedy. Nonetheless, there are things that Christian individuals, families, and communities can and should do. I will speak of these things in light of my previous reflections regarding the Benedict Option.

Of course, any thought of the Benedict Option as an opportunity for living in some of form of "splendid isolation", self-sufficient, distant, and therefore safe from the fray, is a dangerous fantasy. No one can escape from the conflict. We are all already involved and affected. The question remains: Going forward, how shall we live?

It seems to me that as we evaluate any claims of a Benedict Option, we must first heed Esolen's exhortation to "get out of the sewer." With that in mind, let us consider the following:

1. Granted that most of us cannot lessen significantly our living *in* the world, what can we do to lessen the degree that we are *of* the world?
2. What can we do, short-term, mid-term, long-term, to ensure that we can perform both the spiritual and corporal works of mercy?
3. What can we do, short-term, mid-term, long-term, to ensure that the powers of and treasures of true faith and right reason are handed on, intact, to the next generation?
4. How shall we do all of the above in a context of increasing distress, crisis, adversity, opposition, deprivation, and danger? (As I write these words, I recall

when I was invited, as a new priest, to speak to students about "spirituality as an aspect of wellness". Ha!)

Regarding the first point, I think of one of the Desert Fathers, Saint Arsenius the Great, who advised, "Flee, pray always, be silent, for these are the sources of sinlessness." How shall a Jesuit, as a son of Saint Ignatius Loyola, understand and live those words? Let us walk through the wisdom of those words slowly and carefully.

FLEE: From what would I be fleeing? About a year ago, I published these words—"Flee from what distracts you, addicts you, seduces you, deceives you, entices you. Flee from what would take all from you and give you nothing, and less than nothing." It sounds like what we should be fleeing from can be brought to us by just about any electronic medium, does it not? It sounds like everything that John Senior warned us about in his wise diagnostic book *The Death of Christian Culture*. We must flee from whatever will dim our intellect, weaken our will, dull our senses.

And what should we be fleeing toward? In that same essay, I wrote—"Flee toward what will nourish you, heal you, enlighten you, enliven you. Flee toward what will liberate you, elevate you, and perfect you." I stand by those words and would summarize by saying, "Flee to what will sanctify you."

BE SILENT: Why? Silence has been reflected upon across cultures and millennia. It is more urgent than ever to ask and answer the question, "Why be silent?" We must do so because so many of our contemporaries would find any praise of silence to be either risible or incomprehensible. Worse, I fear, are those who would find the call to silence to be terrifying. So many would not know what to do with themselves in the presence of silence. And, sad to say, there are some who would rather die than be alone with their thoughts, for fear of what they might hear.

Yes, there are times when we would do well to "get away from it all." For most of us, such opportunities are rare, if not outright impossible. (At this moment, I cannot help but think of a poor friend who has been pining to go on a silent retreat for years. Every time she has booked a retreat, as the day draws near, disaster strikes—blizzards, civil unrest, power outages, plagues, etc. We have joked that if she actually makes it to a retreat house, a comet will hit the planet, and it will be her fault.)

Even so, a place of physical silence and solitude, however beneficial, would not be enough. We must find, deep within ourselves, a sanctuary, a citadel of the soul, if you will, accessible no matter where our body may be. Secure in that citadel of inner silence, we may be able to hear, if we are attentive, the one "still small voice" that we have in fact been longing to hear, the voice we were made for (see 1 Kings 19:11–13). I wrote elsewhere that such silence "cannot be found if you are defenseless against the chaos around you and all-too-tolerant of the chatter within you."

PRAY ALWAYS: Our Lord did not say, "Pray more" or "Pray better." In Luke 18:1, we read that he urged us "always to pray and not lose heart". It would be out of place here to launch into a full exegesis of that text. For our purposes here and now, I will just say that we cannot "always pray and not lose heart" if we have no experience of and no desire for exterior and interior silence.

Let us reach back to the second point to be considered in this meditation, namely, ensuring that we will be able to perform both the spiritual and corporal works of mercy. There is a great deal that has been said regarding these works of mercy, both individually and collectively. I need not reproduce any of that there. Instead, I want to reflect on the necessity of having individuals and communities alike be prepared to perform *both* the spiritual and the corporal works of mercy. It is true that an individual or community might have a preference or even a charism for either the spiritual or corporal works. Fair enough. I will explain briefly how the two species of works are related. More importantly, I want to show how we might be prepared for both sets of works in order to be good stewards during the time of disorder, disruption, and disaster that is unfolding before us.

We have bodies. We are susceptible to hunger, thirst, and the elements. Yet we are not mere animals. Made in the image and likeness of God, we are able with our immaterial and immortal souls to know and will. We are made for Truth, Goodness, and Beauty. Fallen creatures, we are susceptible to error and vice. We need care of body and soul together; we must learn how to offer both.

Especially in the West, there has been a trend to move the family from being a place of production to a place of consumption. So many these days can scarcely cook food, much less grow it. Our delivery of life's necessities to a modern urban area is staggeringly complex and frightfully fragile. How will Christians care for each other's material needs if the times suddenly and significantly become leaner and meaner?

My point can perhaps be illustrated by a scene from the post-apocalyptic novel, *Alas, Babylon*, by Pat Frank, published in 1959. As I recall the scene, a woman is at the kitchen sink washing dishes when in the distance she sees a mushroom cloud. She says to herself in response, "Well, that can't be good. I should probably pick up some extra groceries tomorrow. I wonder where I left my check-book?" And then she goes back to washing dishes.

I like to tell that story in order to illustrate the power of "normalcy bias", that is, to focus on the familiar and routine, to the point where we are unable to imagine or perceive what is out-of-the-ordinary.

Our normalcy bias tells us that the local grocery store will always have groceries and that the local parish will always offer the sacraments. We are not inclined to think about how groceries or the sacraments got to where we could reach them. And we certainly do not like to plan for what to do when the groceries and sacraments are not to be found in their usual and convenient locations. But we must do so if we are to be faithful stewards of Christ in these increasingly chaotic times.

I will leave those more qualified than I to guide you in preparing to provide life's physical necessities. My concern here and now is to stimulate reflection, prayer, study, conversation, and *action*, so that Catholics are prepared to remain faithful and fruitful disciples in difficult, perhaps even extreme conditions.

An interesting example to consider would be the amazing history of the *Kakure Kirishitan*, the "Hidden Christians" of Japan. In brief: Christian missionaries became active in Japan around 1549. The Christian community grew quickly. Tragically, there was a brutal persecution of Christians and, finally, an expulsion of foreign missionaries around 1614.

The missionaries promised to return someday. They gave instructions to the Japanese laity about how to discern the authenticity of future missionaries. These must be celibate, loyal to the pope, and honor the Virgin Mary. More than 250 years later, the missionaries returned and were surprised to find underground Christians who said to the missionaries, "The hearts of all of us here do not differ from yours." (The clarity and pristineness of doctrine that was found among them is a complicated story, better told by someone more qualified than I.)

The moral of that story, for our purposes, is to note that the Japanese Christians chose to persevere, for generations, in conditions so extreme as to defy our comprehension. What do we think we would need to persevere, to hand on the faith intact, to keep alive the spirit and content of Catholic intellectual life, if the usual institutional supports, so often taken for granted, were unexpectedly diminished, compromised, or inaccessible?

As a Jesuit, I know that there is a noble and blood-soaked history of "recusant" Catholics, starting in the England of Henry VIII. These stalwart souls kept the faith, hid priests, and met clandestinely for prayer and worship. That noble and poignant chapter of Catholic history is being relived in China today.

As I write this, I am restricted to offering Mass only out-of-doors, under unusual conditions, because of what I have called "the Covid Interruption" or "the Season of Covidtide" or "the reign of King Covid". My purpose is not to pronounce on the putative dangers of Covid or the putative merits of the various responses to the virus.

I write this knowing that for the first time in American history, Easter was "cancelled" and that Christmas is in doubt. We have all just lived through the inconceivable. That should spark our imagination as we prepare for the future.

MEDITATION XXXII: The Beginning of the End? Or the End of the Beginning?

It has been a while since I have last taken up my pen. I would have liked to have finished the first draft of this manuscript by now. I am surrounded by distractions and interruptions; I must admit that I have not been managing them well.

I find myself caught between the perennial and the passing. The passing includes the election and post-election madness of recent weeks and months. The perennial dimension is made salient to me by the fact that we are in the midst of the Christmas season.

I want to avoid the trite and cheap sentimentality associated with Christmas—especially the more secular approaches to the season. Christmas, properly understood and celebrated, is akin to the recollection of the start of a great military campaign. The great Allied landing in Normandy on D-Day in World War II comes to mind. Was it not at D-Day that Winston Churchill said, "This may not be the beginning of the end, but it is the end of the beginning"?

It is a paradox, is it not? The Incarnation and Nativity of Our Lord constitute elements of the absolute victory of the Christ of God. Admittedly, from our perspective, in time the victory is not fully realized. Or is it better to say that the victory is not fully manifest to *us*? How can human moral agents live through time lucidly, as they discern the passing, the perennial, and the eternal?

We are in fact invited to participate in the battle of light versus darkness, of *Logos* versus chaos. We are given the privilege of standing beside Christ, taking up His fight against the dark. Those who persevere will share in His victory and His glory. How shall this fact and promise guide us during the storm heading toward us?

MEDITATION XXXIII: Merely Human?

What does it mean to be an "ordinary person"? May a Christian rightly speak of being "merely human"? To the second question, I believe that a Christian must say, "No." If a Christian is acquainted with C. S. Lewis, then the Christian must answer the question with a resounding, "No!" Lewis would say that we humans, each human, will become either a celestial treasure or a diabolical horror, a tale of triumph or of tragedy. A well-formed Christian knows that a human, even a human on this side of the grave, cannot be "merely human".

What about being an "ordinary human"? I think that "human" in this sense can be understood in a variety of ways. "Ordinary human", if taken to be merely human, must, as seen above, be dismissed by the faithful Christian. I think then that we are left with understanding "ordinary human" as being either normative or typical. Let us look at the latter first.

How to describe an ordinary human as "typical"? I recall a Peanuts cartoon from my childhood. Lucy asks Schroeder to tell her a story. He recites, "A man was born. He lived and died. The end." That account may be thought of as "typical" because it is true of every human. Yet Lucy's response poses a challenge: "Kind of makes you wish you knew the guy." The problem is that this account, which is universal, if taken as total, will stifle curiosity and wonder. Just as it is true (and made true by quite deliberate and strenuous effort) that if "you've tasted one can of Pepsi, you've tasted them all", so too, on this account of human nature, it is true that "If you've met one human, you've met them all."

But what if there is more to be said of humans besides "They are born and later they die"? What if there were more to human nature than a finite span linking birth and death? This line of inquiry faces two directions—it faces universality and particularity.

Regarding the universal: A well-formed and well-informed Christian knows that all human persons are made in the image and likeness of God. We are rational, free, and moral. By virtue of the Incarnation of the Christ of God, we fallen humans, composed of body and soul, made for infinite Truth, Goodness, and Beauty, offered salvation and sanctification, have a nature that may be perfected by grace. So understood, an ordinary person lives in harmony with his nature as embodied intelligent freedom and strives to cooperate with the elevation, perfection, and completion that only grace can offer. Not surprisingly, then, such an ordinary person, a normal person, a normative person, is rare, even though the fact of human nature and the perfectibility by grace apply to all humans.

"Ordinary person" must also be considered in terms of particularity, of individuality. We must explore this sense of "ordinary person" for the sake of this present project of life in a "post post-Christian age". What is a person, as human as any person, yet unique, unrepeatable, irreducibly precious, to do in a world wherein much or most of Christian culture is inaccessible? What is a truly human and unique individual person to do in a darkening world, when he knows that he has received the light of Christ?

From time to time, I am asked by some friends, "Is it time to panic yet?" My answer so far, and even as I write this, is, "No, it's not time to panic." And it is certainly not ever time to despair. It *is* certainly time—and past time—to give up denial, naïveté, wishful thinking, normalcy bias, and any form of theological presumption.

It is never a failure or error to do the legitimate duties of one's state in life, to the best of one's abilities, with great life. It is never a failure or error to strive with all the help of nature and grace to become free from sin, vice, falsehood, addiction, illusion, or seduction.

Human dignity, human grandeur, a human nature shot through with divinity—all these are offered to the disciples of Christ by their Incarnate Lord. True God and true man, Jesus Christ, who is the light, has overcome darkness, sin, and death. He offers us a matchless nobility, that is, a nobility that the finite and fallen world cannot give or overcome or even understand, by inviting us to fight at His side. Those who bear His Cross will wear His crown. What if we believed that? What if we believed that as individuals and families, as communities small and great? What then? How would our lives be different from how we have lived them, remembered them, imagined them? What if Christians attempted to build cultures or a civilization upon the truth that Christ calls His disciples about Him beneath the banner of His Cross?

And what if in our time, we were called by Christ to be His battle companions just as the ordinary certainties and civilities that so many of us have grown accustomed to receded out of reach and out of sight? What then?

MEDITATION XXXIV: Caesar, Court Jesters, and the Churchians

As I write this, I am aware of erupting change and subtle but firm continuity. Regarding change: across the globe, there are political convulsions—regimes collapsing, contested elections, those who once enjoyed power or celebrity now vilified, demonized, banished, or otherwise "cancelled". (But that is not really news, is it? Perhaps the scope and pace of the changes, along with the scope and pace of the awareness of the changes, are what is different.)

Yet there is continuity. Propagandists lie to the masses. The world, the flesh, and the devil work to ensnare the weak and the strong. And human elements of the Church (what I have referred to here as "the Business of Churchianity" or the *Status Quo Ordo*, or what Muggeridge decried as "Christendom") is once again assuring Caesar that a follower of Christ can be a very useful friend.

As I write this, many millions are celebrating or lamenting the apparent power of elections. Those celebrating, on their own account, are looking forward to witnessing the right people doing the right things. Meanwhile, those being celebrated are making clear (yet again) that they know who their *real* friends are.

What about those lamenting? They seem to be coalescing around various slogans. One group I call the "Let's Be Gracious Losers" Faction. Their answer to the question, "What should we do now?" seems to be, "We'll just do better next time." Critics of this faction are inclined to respond sardonically, noting that shouting, "Government is the problem—VOTE HARDER!" simply cannot be a winning strategy.

These critics can be placed under the umbrella heading of "Going Galt". Consciously or not, they seem to take their inspiration from John Galt, a character in Ayn Rand's novel *Atlas Shrugged*. Galt, as I understand the story, decided to stop "feeding the beast". He absented himself from the cycles of production and taxation that forged the chains of his own oppression.

Very few people, I believe, can live *fully* "off the grid"—assuming that is even possible. Instead, the larger and more realistic "Galt Faction" speaks of "building your own". That is, building apart from the present reigning paradigm and attendant structures separate (alternative? parallel? better?) structures/sources of, say, social media platforms, culture, economy, travel, communities, etc.

This movement itself is critiqued by yet another faction, one we might call the "Political Pragmatists"; they might call themselves the "Realists". Their objection to the Galt

Faction is: "A market solution alone cannot be enough. *We* must have *our* hands on the levers of power, or *they* will. And government has become so pervasive that no lasting and meaningful good change can come unless the right hands hold the reins of the State."

I think that this list of factions need not be considered exhaustive. It can be safely said of these factions that they offer elements of truth and that their advocates may be sincere and well-intentioned. One could have honest disagreement with these factions, individually and collectively. But there is a faction (or perhaps, better said, a genus of factions) that concerns me greatly. The generic label I would apply to these is, "You've God a Friend in Jesus!" The advocates of these factions represent "Christendom" in the pejorative sense rightly decried by Muggeridge.

I want to proceed cautiously and modestly, with an unfeigned humility. Humility is rooted in the truth. The truth is that I am not without sin and have no right to cast stones. I cannot read souls; much less can I judge them. Nor can I do much more than speculate about the sincerity or motivations of others, while entrusting all to God's mercy. Yet humility also requires me to confess that I can and should read words, observe actions, and make inferences. I am a competent student of human nature and human history. I have access to the natural law and the perennial teaching of the Catholic Church.

Consequently, I can draw reasonable conclusions such as, "This bodes well" or "This bodes ill." Likewise, I can reasonably draw conclusions such as, "This is in harmony with what the Church has always taught", or "This is not in harmony with what the Church has always taught."

And, to the best of my ability (such as it is), I try to live up to the good example set by my late, beloved mentor, Dr. Paul Weiss, who said that a good philosopher should be as ready to receive correction as he is to ready to receive vindication. Therefore, if the following observations and inferences need correction, I declare here and now that I will gladly receive that correction. I simply want to know the truth so that I may tell the truth.

My research and observations lead me to say the following about the "You've Got a Friend in Jesus!", or, more simply, the "Friendly Jesus Faction": For over fifty years, the Business of Churchianity as a "brand" has been in steady and steep decline demographically, financially, and culturally. When I use the word "culturally" in this context, I am referring both to the quality of culture produced by Churchianity as well as to the degree of influence that Churchianity exercises in popular culture.

Regarding the status of Christ in the present mass culture, try this as a thought experiment. Can you really and readily imagine creators and purveyors of popular culture today saying, "We can't do that! It might offend the Christians!"

The stewards (or, perhaps better said, "the owners and operators") of Churchianity—for convenience's sake, let us call them the "Churchians"—know that their brand is fading. They also know that they have lots of infrastructure to support and a payroll to maintain. The cash flow for Churchians is now merely trickling. What to do?

Even a casual observer can see that the State has access to a lot of money. And an astute observer will note that politics is downstream from culture. Consequently, it should not be surprising if the Churchians rearrange their brand to appeal to Caesar and the Court Jesters. In other words, the Churchians are for sale, to gain access to the wedding of Bread and Circuses. Caesar manages the distribution of Bread; the Court Jesters manage the Circuses.

Is it too cynical to suggest that the State buys votes by pretending to be Santa Claus? The Churchians, observing that dynamic, see that their interests can overlap with the interests of Caesar. What does that look like?

The Churchians have outsourced the financing of the corporal works of mercy to the State. The Churchians offer to be a reliable broker of the State largesse used to buy votes. After they take their cut, the Churchians can tell themselves and others (and perhaps even God—I do not know) that they are doing God's good work by helping to redistribute wealth appropriated (some would say "confiscated") by the State.

What the Churchians appear to fail to apprehend (as far as I can tell) is that although from time to time the interests of Churchianity and Caesar overlap, they do not correspond. There are conflicting interests in play. Caesar does not give his gold out of the goodness of his heart; he gives only to serve his purposes. Caesar's gold always comes with a cost—a cost sometimes hidden and sometimes not, but there is always a cost.

Apparently, the Churchians have not yet been made fully aware of two awful and practical truths: (1) Caesar holds all the cards; (2) Caesar does not like to be disappointed. As a result of those two truths, the Churchians will have to conform more and more to the will of Caesar, or they will no longer receive his coin, to which they have become tragically and perhaps even fatally addicted.

What about the Court Jesters who manage popular culture? The Churchians want to win the favor of the Court Jesters as well. This is so both for a "hard" reason as well as for a "soft" reason.

The hard reason has to do with demographics and finances. The Court Jesters are the arbiters of what is in favor and what is not. The Churchians believe that if the Court Jesters approve of Churchianity, that will result in people in the pews and cash in the coffers. (Whether that surmise or gamble is correct or prudent is another story for another time.) What do the Court Jesters want in return from the Churchians? Above all, they want compromise and imitation.

They expect compromise in terms of faith and morals. In exchange for granting public approval of Churchianity, the Court Jesters expect the Churchians to remove beliefs that the Jesters find incredible or otherwise embarrassing. In terms of compromised morals, the Jesters will offer approval to Churchianity on the condition that the Churchians will praise or censure whatever the Jesters want praised or censured.

Regarding imitation, recall the adage that "imitation is the sincerest form of flattery." And the Court Jesters crave flattery. Churchianity flatters the Jesters especially by adapting worship to imitate the modes of entertainment ascendent in popular culture. So, we see places of worship being rearranged (or even designed!) to function as pop music venues, outsized home entertainment centers, etc. There are many problems with this (eloquently denounced by A. W. Tozer, for example), not the least of which is that this modification of worship is done so risibly and tragically badly. Churchianity cannot match, much less exceed, the worldliness of the world. Churchianity's budget, ingenuity, and technical skills will always fall short of their unambiguously secular counterparts. I will sum up my view of this dynamic (admittedly tongue-in-cheek) with an observation made by social critic Hank Hill: "It's not that you're making church better—you're making rock-and-roll worse."

So much for the "hard" reason to seek out the approval of the Court Jesters. What of the "soft" reason? The soft reason is rooted in a simple and inescapable fact: Churchians are human! As human as you and I. We humans delight in praise and cringe at criticism. And the Court

Jesters are quite well able to make widely known both their praise and their criticism.

Whom the Court Jesters celebrate become celebrities; whom they scorn become pariahs. Together, the Court Jesters are a fickle lot. They can switch from cheers to jeers without warning or explanation. And like Caesar, they do not respond well to disappointment.

Where do all these observations leave us? And where might they lead us? It would be unseemly, I think, for a Jesuit to recommend the digging of catacombs or the construction of an ark. Besides, really, there is no place to run, no place to hide, no way of living that will exempt us from unwelcome scrutiny, truly inconvenient truths, and awkward questions. A response is required of us. Caesar and the Court Jesters will demand a response. So will God. How shall we respond? For now, I will say this much: We will need both innovation (which is not mere novelty) and tradition (which is not mere archaism).

MEDITATION XXXV: "You Can't Turn Back the Clock"

I have been thinking a good deal lately about history. In doing so, I recall the many times I have heard the admonition, "You can't turn back the clock." I find this statement to be as obvious as it is unhelpful. ("You can't be more Catholic than the pope" is equally obvious and unhelpful, although, of course, for different reasons.) No one seriously suggests turning back the clock. Time cannot be rewound; history, although it can be forgotten, obscured, or rewritten, cannot be undone. Surely, people who say that "you can't turn back the clock" do not intend to communicate, "It's impossible to learn from experience." They do not mean to say that, but that is what their words connote, if not actually denote.

As I began to write this work, I knew from the outset that it would not include a call to return to any "Good Old Days". There were none. I am not suggesting a "turning back the clock" or the refurling of the calendar to a "better time", however one might define "better" or "time".

Of course, I do believe that we can and should learn from history, even going so far as to make great efforts to retrieve wisdom, practices, and artifacts from the past. And I do intend to discuss in these pages the what, how, and why of such retrievals. But first I want to reflect on (fallen) human nature's relationship with history.

This week, I stumbled upon some essays about education, democracy, and equality written by C. S. Lewis. Most of these essays were published over seventy-five years ago. Yet their substance suggests that they could have been written this week, because they articulate so clearly some of our contemporary problems.

Lewis in these essays speaks of pseudo-egalitarianism masquerading as democracy in schools, harming both education and democracy. He discussed the lowering of standards and the emergence of what we today would call "participation trophies". He identifies a cult of sentimentalism that demands the surrender of commitments to standards, merit, excellence, distinction, rank—all in the name of what some would today call (or as Lewis might say, "mislabel") "inclusion".

Please allow me a digression for a moment to speak of the contemporary misapprehension of the words "inclusion" and "exclusion". Such misapprehension, I fear, has already become hallowed, institutionalized, standardized, and mandated.

Is "exclusion" an unconditional evil, beyond redemption, to be denounced, forbidden, and extirpated always and everywhere? Is "inclusion" an unconditional good, unassailable, above reproach, to be praised, promoted, and prescribed, always and everywhere? Let us see.

Should the ignorant and incompetent be excluded from medical practice? Or included? Should the craven and corrupt be excluded from elected office? Or included? I know that we cannot "turn back the clock" regarding the common misapprehensions of inclusion and exclusion. But I do maintain that we need to retrieve a more rational and prudent understanding of these words, however arduous and tedious the task may be. (Here ends the digression.)

Upon reading those essays by Lewis that were written well before I was born, I found myself asking the question, "They didn't learn their lesson, did they?" By "they" in this context, I mean Lewis' audience that was contemporary with him. Clearly, "they" did not follow his advice regarding education. Britain is now much farther along the path about which Lewis warned.

An illustration of that point: A British commentator last year publicly wished that Oxford University researchers would fail in developing a vaccine for COVID-19. She did so, not because of a fear of vaccines in general or for a fondness for COVID in particular. Rather, she was worried that such a notable scientific achievement at Oxford University might contribute to some form of pride among Westerners, Caucasians, and native Britons.

As soon as I responded to Lewis' essay with, "They haven't learned their lesson, have they?", I knew that I must ask an additional question: "We haven't learned our lessons, have we?"

Who is the "we" referred to in the question above? I am addressing here the heirs (and therefore the stewards) of Christendom. These heirs have had bequeathed to them a legacy of true faith and right reason, a noble legacy of achievement in the sciences and the arts. The "we" of Christendom has a long record of reflecting upon and acting upon a call to excellence, virtue, magnanimity, even magnificence. (The "Parable of the Talents" [Mt 25:14–30] comes to mind.) Nonetheless, all the goods corroded by sentimentality, pseudo-egalitarianism, and misapprehended inclusion/exclusion (as described by Lewis in those essays from the 1940s)—that is, all the goods that Lewis sought to preserve and promote in those essays decades ago, are under similar (and worse) attack today.

Anyone whose knowledge of human nature, human history, and divine revelation has been illuminated by Christendom already knows how this kind can end. Saint Augustine in his time, Solzhenitsyn and Cardinal Kung in living memory, along with Cardinal Zen in ours could see the trajectory of the path that we are on.

Our Lord warned: "Apart from me you can do nothing" (Jn 15:5). Poor stewards of Christendom, along with the witting and unwitting enemies of Christendom, as well as those caught in the fevered dreams of utopias and dystopias, keep proving His point.

The lessons that we heirs and stewards of Christendom have failed to learn in recent decades is that we ignore the wisdom, warnings, and works of Christendom at our peril. Wherever Christ's reign is not welcome, sin and death, and the absence of charity that is Hell, will prevail. Always. No honest Christian can ever say: "That was then, this is now. This time, it will be different."

MEDITATION XXXVI: Moving from "Christendom Lost" to "Christendom Found"

What shall we do?

Recently a dear and trusted friend sent me an essay he had written. In it are two quotes, both from secular sources. Taken together, they can help us to see the nature and urgency of the need to move from "Christendom Lost" to "Christendom Found".

The first quote is from Montesquieu: "More states have perished by the violation of their moral customs than by the violation of their laws."

What to make of that observation? Contrary to the misapprehensions that characterized the twentieth century (and, alas, it seems the twenty-first century), Christians must insist that politics, narrowly defined as the machinations and manipulations of the apparatus of the State, is not man's noblest endeavor, not his highest good. States and empires, kingdoms and communes—these come and go. A deeper look at human nature will disclose that man is moral, and this even before he makes any legal arrangements. Moreover, he has a transcendent destiny that is not fully realized this side of the grave.

There cannot be any lasting justice or peace if man's moral nature is ignored, subordinated, or denied. Similarly, the human person, both individually and communally, is fated to frustration and failure if the spiritual dimension of human nature is not rightly reckoned with. Simply put— worthy heirs of Christendom always know that there are two, and only two, alternatives: Christ or chaos.

Knowing that, what are good stewards of Christendom to do? Consider this second quote, which is taken from Gustav Mahler, sent to me by my learned friend: "Tradition is not the worship of ashes but the preservation of fire."

That quote is important for our purposes here, and I will address it presently, but first I wish to offer some reassurances. I want to be undeserving of any charge that I am a hopeless (or, perhaps worse, hopeful) romantic, pining for a place and time that never was or can be. I want to be underserving of the charge that I am indulging in a caricature of the worse kind of nostalgia. I certainly want to be underserving of any charges of "restorationism" or "fussy archaism". No. What I want to do is be part of the preservation of fire, the handing on (i.e., the *traditio*) of fire—the holy fire that is Christendom at its best. Regardless of the outcome of the preservation and tradition of the fire of Christendom, I want us to make the effort to preserve and bequeath because it is the right thing to do. We already know what happens if we do not try at all or if we try halfheartedly or halfwittedly.

As I write these words, I want to emphasize that I am not offering a program, an agenda, a structure for new institutions. True, we must not do nothing. True, we must do something. And truly, we must not do merely anything or merely something. We must start with the truth, which is to say that we must start with humility.

With humility, we present heirs of Christendom must confess that we have not been exemplary stewards of the treasures entrusted to us by Christ and His Church. I am thinking of the conclusion of the parable of the servants from Luke 17:7–10: "When you have done all that is commanded you, say, 'We are unworthy servants; we have only done what was our duty.'" Have we done even that?

Contrition, confession, and conversion follow upon true humility. And let us keep in mind Psalm 127:1, "Unless the LORD builds the house, those who build it labor in vain." We will do our best if we do what God asks of us.

A distinction may be helpful here: "Working for God" vs. "Doing God's Work". With the former, we decide what we will do and then ask (or perhaps even demand) that God bless the work. In contrast, the latter depends upon divine initiative. God chooses the work for us, which we accept in obedience, while humbly and trustingly asking for what we need to do the job to the best of our ability.

I believe that doing our best in our time and place includes working as good and faithful stewards of Christendom. We can and should readily admit that we are unlikely instruments and unprofitable servants; at the same time, let us take the focus off ourselves. Let us put our hands to the work while keeping alert to the Master who entrusted the task to us.

MEDITATION XXXVII: Reconnections

Doing God's work entails looking at the past, present, and future. Looking to the past, we must recover or, better said, discover or rediscover much that was displaced or misplaced in recent decades. Christendom's moral and artistic treasures need to be placed before us again. These efforts of discovery and recovery will include remembering and retelling the great lessons of revelation and Church history. We must learn again how to present with confidence, rigor, and charm the truths about, for example, good and evil, virtue and vice, man and woman, Church and State. We can bring refreshment and delight to a weary and jaundiced people through retrieving, as well as by producing anew, what is beautiful.

After the recent trauma of Covidian isolation, we would do well to insist again on the necessities and opportunities for friendship, family, and community life. Would it not be wonderful to be able to give concrete testimony to the joys of being members of the Body of Christ?

I have no prefabricated recipe or formulas readily available for any of the above. Subsidiarity and practical wisdom will be needed at each level and facet of community. Our decisions and commitments in the present are more likely to be fruitful if we take the trouble to inquire of the past and converse with our ancestors. We could ask,

"What worked for you? Why did it work? What can you teach us? What have we forgotten? What do you think we have been getting wrong?" Let us have the good sense to ask these questions of Christendom's past.

One way of viewing the present is to think of it as the intersection of the past and the future. Josef Pieper, if memory serves, warned against a "pastless present" leading to a "groundless hope". The danger of a pastless present that robs and poisons the future is one of the many reasons why the heirs and stewards of Christendom must resist the erasure of the past.

Our debt to the past begins to be paid when and as we secure Christendom for the future. What if we asked: "How shall we live now so that our posterity will bless us rather than curse us?" How might our priorities and aspirations differ from what they are now if we urgently asked ourselves that question daily?

When talking about the future, I am very much inclined to proceed with caution. I am not one to make detailed predictions; much less am I inclined to use the word "prophetic" when speaking of the future.

I can say with confidence that because we have a debt to our forebears, we have an obligation to our posterity. Because we have received so much, we must "pay it forward". What we have received as an inheritance we must secure and transmit.

I remember years ago being saddened by some observations made by George Weigel in his book *The Cube and the Cathedral*. Commenting on the birth dearth in Europe after World War II, he wondered how Western Europeans living in a context of extraordinary peace and prosperity elected not to have children. Apparently, they saw themselves as a people who had nothing to give to the future. Confident heirs and prudent stewards of Christendom would not choose to respond to the past, present, and future in that manner.

MEDITATION XXXVIII: Giving Our Past to Our Future

One of the glories of marriage is the couple's attitude and disposition toward each other and the future when they bring children into the world. In effect, husband and wife say to each other: "I love you so much that I want you to continue, body and soul. And so I will beget children with you and raise them with you, so that you can continue into the future, even beyond your lifespan. The world will be a better place if it can, through our children, see and love in them what I see and love in you. I want the world to see your features and your goodness through the gift of your children."

Could a family, speaking analogously of course, not make a similar statement to its ancestors? Could a family not act so as to make available to the future the customs, stories, and wisdom of previous generations? And could something similar not be done by a clan, tribe, or nation?

If so, could not Christians similarly address the past and future? Having received Christendom from saints, warriors, poets, scholars, mystics, martyrs, missionaries, from artists and artisans, from untold generations of "ordinary" people who secured and handed on Christendom—could we not—should we not—prove our gratitude by imitating our ancestors' fidelity, generosity, and providence?

Having rightly received and addressed our past, cannot we—should not we—the heirs and stewards of Christendom, address and engage the future? Let us ask ourselves a hard, hard question: If future generations had to judge us—right now—on how well we have prepared to hand on Christendom to them, what would their verdict be? Would they thank us for our tenacious fidelity? Our sacrificial generosity? Our stubborn love? Or would they condemn us for handing on to them only the husk of Christendom, and not its substance?

As a young priest, I was asked to attend a meeting of Catholic ecumenists. I did not know what to expect. Even so, I was very much surprised when I was told that now it is time for the Catholic Church to "sit in silence at the feet of the world's religions." I asked those in attendance if they could identify just one thing that the Church ought to say to the world's religions before going silent at their feet. They could not think of anything. I never went back.

How is it possible that the heirs and stewards of Christendom see themselves as having nothing to say to the world, nothing to give to the future, owing nothing to the past? How did this happen? I have some hunches and surmises, but I have no interest in pointing an accusing finger here. Instead, I want to focus on how we can go forward better, bringing the past up from our present and into the future. In doing so, I am mindful of Belloc's observation: "He does not die who does bequeath."

MEDITATION XXXIX: The First Principle and Foundation

One can readily see that the present heirs and stewards of Christendom have profound obligations to the past and to the future. I would go farther: We have debts that on our own we cannot pay. We do not have the wisdom or goodness to satisfy the rightful demands of the past and future upon us. What to do?

We must not do nothing. And we dare not undertake mad initiatives to "fix" things according to our own lights. We do not need another tower of Babel; much less do we need another "City of Man", albeit one with a religious façade. What, then, shall we do?

Previously, I referred to Psalm 127:1: "Unless the LORD builds the house, those who build it labor in vain." Let us dig more deeply into that verse.

It is true that if we would do God's work (rather than "working for God", as discussed earlier), we must learn to listen for the Master's voice, learn to know His ways, so that we might learn to act wisely and well, as heirs and stewards of Christendom. That kind of docility takes generosity, humility, persistence, and magnanimity.

Let us recall, too, that, "Every one to whom much is given, of him will much be required" (Lk 12:48). More is required of us than we are now—humanly speaking—able to give. To become faithful heirs and provident stewards of Christendom will require of us a fundamental reorientation of our lives. It will require a recalibration of our habits of thinking, feeling, and acting. It will require a deep and lasting conversion aimed toward an absolute priority. The Gospel images of Mary of Bethany choosing "the good portion" (Lk 10:42), the farmer finding "treasure hidden in a field" (Mt 13:44), the merchant finding "one pearl of great value" (Mt 13:45–46) come to mind.

What is needed is for us to find the basis for a program of life that is sustained by ongoing conversion and driven by proper priority and urgency. What is needed can be found, I believe, at the outset of Saint Ignatius Loyola's *Spiritual Exercises*, namely, his "First Principle and Foundation".[1]

---

[1] All quotations from Saint Ignatius' Spiritual Exercises have been taken from Louis J. Puhl, S.J., *The Spiritual Exercises of St. Ignatius Based on Studies in the Language of the Autograph* (1951; Chicago: Loyola Press, 1968), no. 23, p. 12.

Saint Ignatius writes: "Man is created to praise, reverence, and serve God our Lord, and by this means to save his soul." His vision recognizes that we Christians are in the world but not of the world. We live in time and space and ought to do so in a way that recognizes the claims made upon us by God who is beyond time and space.

Saint Ignatius continues: "The other things on the face of the earth are created for man to help him in attaining the end for which he is created."

That created natural order in which we find ourselves is made good by God and made useful for man. Yet this world is not our true home. We may rightly use and enjoy the natural order. We should do so with an eye toward the end for which we were made by God, which is eternal communion with Him. Therefore, Saint Ignatius stipulates: "Hence, man is to make use of them in as far as they help him in the attainment of his end, and he must rid himself of them in as far as they prove a hindrance to him."

Note the clarity and practicality of Saint Ignatius' wisdom. He tells us to use what is useful and to distance ourselves from what is distracting or deleterious. Saint Ignatius is, to use contemporary parlance, "in it to win it". He has taken to heart (and hand) the Pauline exhortation to "run that you may [win the race]" (1 Cor 9:24). For our purposes here, this would mean doing whatever is necessary for us to know, love, and hand on Christendom properly. With that commitment comes the necessity to withdraw ourselves from whatever might keep us from that good work.

Then Saint Ignatius begins to specify: "Therefore, we must make ourselves indifferent to all created things, as far as we are allowed free choice and are not under any prohibition. Consequently, as far as we are concerned, we should not prefer health to sickness, riches to poverty, honor to dishonor, a long life to a short life. The same holds for all other things. Our one desire and choice should be what is more conducive to the end for which we are created."

What Saint Ignatius wrote in his "Spiritual Exercises" reflected his own experience of the total reorientation and recalibration of his own life. He rejected, of course, all that is sinful. Yet he appraised with a very keen and critical eye anything ordinarily good in itself. If any good thing distracted him from his goal, he saw that he was obliged to put it out of his life. Similarly, any ordinarily good thing that did not facilitate the achievement of his goal he treated as a luxury that he could not afford.

How does Saint Ignatius' First Principle and Foundation bring light to those who would live as wise and provident heirs and stewards of Christendom? For now, let us look at this question as it may apply to an individual. In the next meditation, we will look at how it may apply to communities.

The First Principle and Foundation can be employed by an individual, insofar as it is based on truths about God and man. At the risk of oversimplifying: God created each man with a purpose. Man succeeds or fails, *qua* man, to the degree that he fulfills that purpose. A wise man will arrange *every* aspect, *every* last detail of his life so as to facilitate his *telos*, the end for which he was made. The First Principle and Foundation, then, is a divinely ordained teleological mandate. It is enjoined upon each and every human person. Any person can embrace it; every person should embrace it.

Reading the First Principle and Foundation, I can say: "This applies to me, as a universal, insofar as I am a human person. Equally, it applies to me uniquely, insofar as I am this particular individual human person. I must apply this universal, that is, I must situate it within the context of my own distinctive life circumstances. These include, say, my state in life, my age and health, my resources, my education, etc." (That list is meant to be illustrative rather than exhaustive.)

The First Principle and Foundation announces and illuminates the task of enacting true freedom in my life—both negative freedom and positive freedom. Negative freedom is freedom-*from*. It entails an unencumbering. Negative freedom entails a purging of illusions, addictions, seductions—any and all disorders that hinder one from attaining the end for which one was made.

Positive freedom is freedom-*for*. It is a teleological expansiveness, an orientation and momentum outward toward the end for which one was made. It is exemplified by the virtue of magnanimity.

I happen to have by my elbow a copy of Josef Pieper's *A Brief Reader on the Virtues of the Human Heart*. As always, Pieper is lucid and succinct: "Magnanimity is the expansion of the spirit toward great things; one who expects great things of himself and makes himself worthy of it is magnanimous."

That is an account of magnanimity in terms of generality. Pieper then becomes specific:

> One who is magnanimous completely shuns flattery and hypocrisy, both of which are the issue of a mean heart. The magnanimous person does not complain, for his heart does not permit him to be overcome by an external evil. Magnanimity encompasses an unshakable firmness of hope, a plainly defiant certainty, and the thorough calm of a fearless heart. The magnanimous person submits himself not to the confusion of feelings or to any human being or fate—but only to God.[2]

---

[2] Josef Pieper, *A Brief Reader on the Virtues of the Human Heart*, trans. Paul C. Duggan (San Francisco: Ignatius Press, 1991), pp. 37–38.

Pieper moves from the general to the specific to the individual. Each individual will have to make discernments and prudential judgments about applying the First Principle and Foundation to his own distinctive here-and-now. All are called to conversion. A husband and father will live the particulars of his conversion differently from the conversion of a consecrated religious. A monk will live his conversion differently from that of a missionary. A missionary in China will live his conversion differently from a missionary in America. A missionary in Los Angeles will live his conversion differently from a missionary in Lincoln, Nebraska, and so on, for each particular and unique individual.

I ask, I implore the reader of this work to make those discernments, to enact those prudential judgments that only you can make to reorient and recalibrate your life as the First Principle and Foundation calls for. The teleological process (that is to say, living life for the right goal) of attaining the end for which you were made will include learning to live as a wise and provident heir and steward of Christendom.

If one objects that terms such as "First Principle and Foundation", "magnanimity", or "teleological dynamism" seem painfully abstract, I will (grudgingly) concede the point. Saint Ignatius Loyola will not let us stay at such a level of apparent (*not* "mere") abstraction. He knew how to spark the imagination to spur a lifetime of heroic and generous action. His masterpiece for inducing the birth of holy heroes is the Spiritual Exercises, taken in its entirety. In particular, the meditation of "the Call of the King" can stir magnanimity like nothing else I know. I will leave it to the reader to take the initiative for finding a good guide for that meditation. (*My Path to Heaven*, by Geoffrey Bliss, S.J., is a good place to start.)

For our present purposes, it will suffice to quote just a few lines from the Exercises. Saint Ignatius (like everyone else) was a man of his time. In his context as a Catholic writing in the sixteenth century, he asks us to imagine the obligation one would have to answer the call of a good Christian king. How much more, then, would a person of right reason and good will have to answer the call of Christ the King? Saint Ignatius writes:

> If such a summons of an earthly king to his subjects deserves our attention, how much more worthy of consideration is Christ our Lord, the Eternal King, before whom is assembled the whole world. To all His summons goes forth, and to each one in particular He addresses the words: "It is my will to conquer the whole world and all my enemies, and thus to enter into the glory of my Father. Therefore, whoever wishes to join me in this enterprise must be willing to labor with me, that by following me in suffering, he may follow me in glory."[3]

What Saint Ignatius writes as a worthy response to the summons by Christ the King merits from each Christian a lifetime of contemplation and action:

> Those who wish to give greater proof of their love, and to distinguish themselves in whatever concerns the service of the eternal King and Lord of all, will not only offer themselves entirely for the work, but will act against their sensuality and carnal and worldly love, and make offerings of greater value and of more importance in words such as these:
>
> "Eternal Lord of all things, in the presence of Thy infinite goodness, and of Thy glorious mother, and of all the saints of Thy heavenly court, this is the offering of myself which I make with Thy favor and help. I protest

[3] Puhl, *Spiritual Exercises*, p. 44.

that it is my earnest desire and my deliberate choice, provided only it is for Thy greater service and praise, to imitate Thee in bearing all wrongs and all abuse and all poverty, both actual and spiritual, should Thy most holy majesty deign to choose and admit me to such a state and way of life."[4]

Good and generous souls who make such an offering will be transformed. They can be truly free, so free as to be able to retrieve the treasure that is Christendom, and hand it on to the next generation.

MEDITATION XL: The Dangerous Liaisons of Church and State

In recent meditations here we have been reflecting on how an individual might live wisely and well as an heir and steward of Christendom. Let us spend some time now on how the same might be done by communities. And I want to do so by noting first certain features of the cultural and political contexts in which so many Christian communities find themselves nowadays. It has been said that "Politics is downstream from culture", so let us start with culture.

I seem to recall some years ago that a prominent church-man declared in a televised interview, "The culture war is over." Upon hearing that, I thought, "That's odd. I don't remember receiving my invitation to the victory parade. I wonder if it got lost in the mail?"

My musings continued: "If the culture war is over—who won?" I can easily hear the collective voice of my more cynical friends saying, "Who won the culture war? Let me help you with that—it was not Christendom."

[4] Ibid., 44–45.

Here is my checklist as I consider whether the culture war is over:

1. Are there cultural elements worth defending? Yes. Are they still under attack? Yes. Then the culture war is not over.
2. Are there cultural elements worth promoting? Yes. Are these being misunderstood, misrepresented, resisted, or replaced? Yes. Then the culture war is not over.
3. Is Christendom (in the best sense of the word) flourishing? No. Is Christ the King known and loved by all? No. Then the culture war is not over.

In short, the culture war cannot be over until Christ returns in glory.

I have said before in these pages that since the French Revolution, the West has earnestly sought to organize public and private life without reference to Christ. Since then, the scope and momentum of Western Civilization have moved from a separation from Christ to a repudiation of Christ and of Christians. Here, some may interject and say that I am overstating the case. I answer that my words are not hyperbolic; nor do I think that they are unreasonable or intemperate. I readily admit that not everyone who is not a happy heir of Christendom is a militant atheist, in the mold, say, of Voltaire or Marx. If only that were the case! It is easier to fight a battle where opponents are all wearing the same uniform and following a readily recognizable flag.

What concerns me (and this is Muggeridge's point regarding the shadowy sense of Christendom) is the inclination of apparent friends of Christendom to disarm, dilute, and denature Christianity itself. Sadly, such anti-Christians find some glad allies among those who have been baptized.

There are more than a few "cultural influencers" who wish to see Christianity be compromised or be silent or be silenced. The goal of Christianity as compromised or silent may be effected by cultural influence. The goal of Christianity as silenced is the work of the State.

The State has had, to be generous, an ambivalent and changing attitude toward Christianity, the Church, Christians, and Christendom. As I look at the sentence above, it occurs to me that although I do not use those words as synonyms, some, perhaps many, people might. Therefore, some distinctions are in order before I continue with my analysis.

In the context of this present work in general, and in the present analysis in this particular meditation, by "Christianity" I refer to the intellectual content and moral meaning of Christ's revelation. This includes the long and storied history of His disciples reflecting on what He has revealed.

In this case, "the Church" refers to the institutional embodiment of Christianity. It is a visible manifestation of the attempts to express and secure in public life the truth and ethics of Christianity. Buildings, jurisdictions, committees, and the like, on this view fall under the heading of "Church".

"Christians" are simply those who have been baptized. So understood, whether fervent or indifferent, each baptized person is a Christian.

By "Christendom" in this context, I refer to a two-sided coin, so to speak, with Muggeridge on one side and Senior on the other. The Muggeridge side represents Christianity's painful (and open) secret: Christendom is an illegitimate child born of the tragic union of Church and corrupted culture, sanctioned by the State.

On the Senior side of the coin, "Christendom" represents the beloved and fruitful cultural progeny born of the Christ-sanctioned matrimony of human nature and divine grace. Some find the lineage of this union to be inspiring. Others find the lineage to be irrelevant. Some see Christendom's heritage as potentially useful, as well as potentially threatening, as "useful" and "threatening" are understood in political and material terms. And, sadly, some find in Christendom an excuse for murderous rage.

Considering all of the above, it is not always easy to sort out the attitudes of the State in relation to the revelation of and followers of Christ, in all of their public and private, individual and communal forms. Even so, I think it is safe to say that since the time of the French Revolution, the State jealously guards its primacy and prerogatives. It does not tolerate rivals and has little patience for divided or uncertain loyalties.

A modern secular State would find a robust, pervasive, confident, and beloved Christendom to be unbearable. Such a Christendom, by its very existence, would highlight the limitations and contradictions inherent in the State's very nature. Moreover, a hardy and mature Christendom would articulate the secular State's most desperate and secret threefold shame:

1. The secular State is not and cannot be inevitable.
2. The secular State is not and cannot be absolute.
3. The secular State will not and cannot endure.

In the view of the secular State, that which is called "Christian", be it Christianity or Church or Christendom, must be corrupted or destroyed. The secular State could never forgive Christendom for knowing and telling the State's threefold fatal shame.

The secular State can apply social pressure on all things Christian, offering flattery for those who cooperate and shunning for those who do not. The secular State, with the enormous and powerful apparatus of law and finance (and these—always—backed ultimately by violence) can make all things Christian into either cattle or criminal.

To undertake even a modest study of the interactions between the secular State and Christendom would be as demanding as it would be illuminating. But, however deep or wide one makes such a study, it suffers from an awkward and unfortunate limitation. You can keep yourself at a safe distance, morally speaking, from what happened in other times and places. As useful and enlightening as these studies may be (and they are), we need to do something different and, if I may say so, something better.

I believe that as Christian individuals and Christian communities, we heirs of Christendom must undertake an examination of conscience. We need an examination of conscience regarding our individual and communal stewardship of Christendom. In particular, we need to look for our sins of commission and omission in terms of how we as Christendom's heirs have interacted with the secular state in our own particular times and places.

Have we embraced or rejected the corruption of Christendom? Have we conceded to the promised blandishments or scorn of mass culture? Have we been won over by the financial enticements or thuggish threats of the secular State?

I write these words on Ash Wednesday, knowing that writing them this day, with the intention of having them published, entails a long and difficult Lent for me. I hope that with God's grace this Lent may be as liberating and as fruitful as it promises to be painful.

MEDITATION XLI: Great Ideas and Big Plans

If good and provident heirs and stewards of Christendom take seriously the observation that both mass culture and the secular State enthusiastically wield all their soft and hard powers against Christians, along with Christians' divine mandate and their divine-human heritage, what is to be done? Should there not be a plan? Preferably a big one? And should that big plan not be led by the great and the good, for the benefit of everyone?

Much earlier in this work, I referred to Alfred Jay Nock's essay "Isaiah's Job". There he warned his readers against listening to anyone who claims to have the one great idea that is going to fix everything. Writing between two world wars, with both fascism and communism getting ready to boil over, one can respect his sense of caution.

Here is an objection: "But isn't it different when the good guys do it? Would it really be a bad thing for the good guys to come up with a great plan for everyone's benefit?"

I answer that the weaknesses inherent in fallen man, along with the incalculable complexities of human inter-actions on a global scale, doom such grand efforts to failure or worse. Perhaps a few quick illustrations will clarify what I mean about the grand plans of the great and the good, as well as the not-so-great and not-so-good.

A few years ago, Alan Jacobs published *The Year of Our Lord 1943: Christian Humanism in an Age of Crisis.* Jacobs looks at the writings and public statements of five sig-nificant figures: W. H. Auden, T. S. Eliot, C. S. Lewis, Jacques Maritain, and Simone Weil. Jacobs' thesis is that by 1943, after America's entrance into the Second World War, allied victory appeared inevitable. The five figures listed above, along with several others reviewed by Jacobs collectively (if not always collaboratively) distilled a diag-nosis and prescription. In sum, the diagnosis of the nearly fatal fever afflicting the world was secular humanism. The prescription was a reclaiming of an earlier Christian humanism. This diagnosis and prescription would not surprise anyone familiar with Hilaire Belloc, who years before had stated, "There are only two alternatives for society ... Christ or chaos."

By the end of the book, the grand plan for securing peace in goodness in the post-World War II world, based on a "restoration of the specifically Christian understanding of the human being"[1] comes to a conclusion that we can readily accept as true. We need the truth about God and the truth about man, and then we need to act accordingly, individually and communally. The saving truth about God and about man is found in the God-man, Jesus Christ. Alas, there was no revival of Christian humanism on a global scale. Yet the disappointing past can still provide guidance for those in the present who are willing to learn. Jacobs notes: "If ever again there arises a body of thinkers eager to renew Christian humanism, they should take great pains to learn from those we have studied here."[2]

Why this failure? Why were there no takers for this plan devised by the great and the good? In part, because that plan was overshadowed by another plan—a plan devised by the not-so-great and the not-so-good.

The story of the rise, fall, and persistence of that subsequent plan is ably summarized in R. R. Reno's book *Return of the Strong Gods: Nationalism, Populism and the Future of the West*. Reno's story resembles the one told by Jacobs. After the global trauma of two world wars, influential and credentialed people offered a diagnosis and prescription.

Herewith the diagnosis: "dogmatic convictions and passionate loyalties" incline individuals and communities toward conflict and war. Populism, nationalism, and

---

[1] Alan Jacobs, *The Year of Our Lord 1943: Christian Humanism in an Age of Crisis* (New York: Oxford Univ. Press, 2018), p. 50.

[2] Ibid., p. 206.

religion—what Reno calls "the strong gods", on this account—have a tragic history of bringing about widespread madness and death.

Thus, the prescription: The "strong gods" can and should be replaced by a way of proceeding that is moderate, tolerant, nominalist, relativist, economic, technological, and scientific. The aim would be to diminish occasions for conflict and promote occasions for cooperation. We can build a peaceful society of great opportunities if we give up the quixotic and tragic quests to build a society of great truths—truths believed by their adherents to be worth dying for and worth killing for.

Reno documents that the "open society" advocated by this grand strategy never really caught on, but, not for lack of trying. Even so, in recent years, in the civil order, nationalist and populist movements are cropping up all over the West. In the spiritual order, traditionalist movements have gained considerable momentum, especially among the young. To the surprise of the planners, the "strong gods" of dogmatic convictions and passionate loyalties are resilient.

The "new secularists", if we may call them that, are not ready to surrender. In fact, they seem to be doubling down. We see this in various programs such as Agenda 21, the Great Reset, Build Back Better, and the like. An intensification of suspicion and conflict seems inevitable.

I would be remiss here if I did not mention the person and work of Pope John Paul II, a landmark figure of the twentieth century. He experienced firsthand the horrors that so many cultural influencers and civil leaders wanted to diagnose and prevent. He witnessed the villainies inflicted by two bloody monsters who embodied the worst of the most confident and militant errors about God and man. He was a forced laborer for the Nazis in German-occupied

Poland. As a bishop, he guarded his flock against the Communist wolves of Soviet-occupied Poland.

His diagnosis of the chief maladies of the twentieth century (namely, secularist distortions of God and man) led to a prescription that the figures of Jacobs' book would endorse: public and private life arranged in light of the Incarnation of Christ the King. The principal difference between his prescriptions and theirs is that he promulgated his while a successor of the Apostles and later as the successor of Saint Peter. He promoted his prescription tirelessly for decades as the most-traveled pope in history.

And now ...? After all of his writing, speaking, and witnessing, sixteen years after his death, where is the prescription of Pope John Paul II being enacted, and by whom? Said another way: As of 2021, is the influence of Pope John Paul II waxing or waning? In the secular world, where is the thought of Pope John Paul II in ascendance? In the Christendom of Muggeridge and the Christendom of Senior, where is his work the animating principle? Admittedly, one could point to small or modest blossoms scattered here and there. But his grand vision of a Christ-centered public order, as far as I can tell on the date that I write this, has not won the day on the global stage.

Perhaps it is time, at least for a while, to put grand visions and plans on a shelf. It may be time, instead, to take the highest Christian aspirations and use modest means to plant holy and humane seeds in local soils.

MEDITATION XLII: Four Strategies

At this point, I can easily imagine a reader saying: "Okay. We can't do nothing. We can't do everything. And attempts at implementing 'The One Big Plan to Fix It All'

have a very poor track record. Maybe we should be thinking and acting on a smaller scale and closer to home. What
would that look like?"

I have heard that good question asked earnestly and often.
Over the years. I have come across many responses. These
can be summarized by four types. These are (1) "Circle
the wagons"; (2) "Build an ark"; (3) "Flee to the catacombs"; (4) *Reconquista* or "Riding forth". Let us review
them in turn.

1. "Circle the wagons." This is a short-term strategy.
   It involves hunkering down, sticking together, and
   waiting for the storm to pass, however one defines
   "storm". Circling the wagons is a way of shelter-
   ing in place until conditions become more favorable.
   The telltale sign of this strategy sounds something
   like this: "Yes, we're taking these extraordinary mea-
   sures, but only temporarily. Once there's a change
   in . . ." And then the statement becomes an exercise
   in fill-in-the-blank: Once there is a new adminis-
   tration, a new governor, a new king, a new bishop,
   a new pope, etc., then we can get back to normal.
   Upon hearing such statements, some are inclined
   to respond with: "I haven't seen 'normal' in a long
   time, and I don't expect normal to come back any
   time soon. We need a different kind of strategy. We
   need, not a short-term, but a mid-term strategy."
2. "Build an ark." This is like option one, but with the
   expectation that the storm may last for a good long
   while. But there is another and perhaps more important difference between these two options. With
   option one, if you do not circle the wagons, you
   might survive but will almost certainly not flourish.
   With option two, you will neither flourish nor survive

outside of the ark. On this view, outside the ark, you will inevitably be swept away by the flood. I think that this option is what Alasdair MacIntyre alluded to at the end of his *After Virtue*. This allusion was fleshed out by Rod Dreher in his *The Benedict Option*.

That book has generated much conversation and publication. Criticism of that book and variations on it abound. (I suppose that my own work here might be considered "A Jesuit Option" or at least "A Jesuit Look at the Benedict Option".) A repeated criticism of the ark strategy is that it may misapprehend the issue of time. This misapprehension has two dimensions.

On this view, the first misapprehension is how long the storm will last. If you stay on an ark long enough, eventually you will run out of everything. The second misapprehension has to do with the proximity of the storm. It takes time to build an ark. Even if all that was necessary for an ark were readily available, some believe that there simply is not enough time to build an ark.

I confess that at this moment, I cannot help but think of a popular meme circulating on the Internet. The caption reads: "If you're gonna fight, fight like you're the third monkey on the ramp to Noah's Ark ... and brother, it's starting to rain." In response, the critics of the ark option would point out that the meme assumes that an ark already exists. It also assumes that it is just "starting" to rain. Ark critics are likely to insist that it has been raining for quite some time, that the river is about to overflow its banks, and that the dam is about to break. What are we to do?

3. "Flee to the catacombs." The concept of the catacombs is rich in imagery in both Christian

iconography and history. In contrast to the first two options, the catacomb strategy can be viewed as a long-term strategy, but with a significant difference. The previous strategies assume that you can stay safe and that the storm will pass before supplies run out. People who flee to the catacombs cannot stay there indefinitely. They cannot even stay there for very long. Catacomb advocates will agree with that observation, while insisting that it misses the point: "Of course we can't survive for long in the catacombs—but we don't need to. We only need to stay away from prying eyes just long enough to do what is so distinctively Christian that it would get us killed aboveground. We come to the catacombs to catechize and worship, but not to live."

In other words, the advocates of the catacombs live most of their lives aboveground. They stay alive by living in such a way that they appear to fit in where they know they do not belong. Their motto might be, "Don't do anything that might attract the guards' attention."

The catacomb advocates strive to be quick-witted and cunning survivors. They hide themselves aboveground, in public, in order to make a living. They go below ground, in private, for teaching, worship, and fellowship. Said another way: they know that for the time being they can only reveal their true selves safely underground. Only in the catacombs dare they remove their masks.

In theory, one can live above and worship below indefinitely. In practice, the catacomb strategy is fraught with peril. One is in constant danger of discovery, betrayal, or compromise. The advocates of the catacombs say that they accept the risk because if they are to remain faithful, they have no alternative. Their critics say there is an alternative yet to be considered.

4. *Reconquista* or "Riding forth". A criticism of the first three strategies may be found in these words of nineteenth-century diplomat Juan Donoso Cortés: "Don't tire yourself in seeking a place of security against the chances of war, for you tire yourself in vain; that war is extended as far as space and prolonged through all time. In eternity alone, the country of the just, can you find rest, because there alone there is no combat."

One could easily imagine a nineteenth-century romantic, or a Cervantes of an earlier age, tearing up at the thought of leading a cavalry charge while crying out: "To glorious victory or honorable death!"

Reconquista or "riding forth" distinguishes itself from the first three strategies by prioritizing victory (or at least defiance) over endurance. The pushing back against the onslaught, as I understand it, calls for a mixture of hope, anger, and courage. Saint Augustine wrote that, "Hope has two beautiful daughters; their names are Anger and Courage. Anger at the way things are and Courage to see that they do not remain as they are."

A truly courageous act is never an act of futility but is done with an openness to a hope for victory. Without righteous anger, without what Saint Thomas Aquinas calls a "just wrath", we will not have the needed energy and endurance to protect the vulnerable and promote the good. Aquinas held that the brave man uses just wrath for his own act, above all in attack, stating: "for it is peculiar to wrath to pounce upon evil. Thus, fortitude and wrath work directly upon each other."

Is that not amazing? Aquinas declares that it is the work of the courageous Christian to "pounce upon evil". Already, one can hear cheers arise from among the ranks of the *Reconquistas*. One can hear among them recitations of our Lord's words in the Gospels: "Unless a grain of wheat falls into the earth and dies" (Jn 12:24); "[whoever] would come after me, let him ... take up his cross" (Mt 16:24); "whoever would save his life will lose it; and whoever loses his life for my sake, he will save it" (Lk 9:24).

Consequently, the *Reconquistas* would accept these words from the book *The God We Seek*, written by my mentor, Paul Weiss, who described himself as an agnostic and a Jew:

> Judaism is one long drawn-out lament; for the Christian this is but the necessary birth-cry of a joyous miracle. The two positions cannot be one, for it is of the essence of Judaism to deny and of Christianity to affirm that there was a day some two thousand years ago in which darkness suddenly and forever gave way to a blinding light. Judaism is Moses in the wilderness straining to reach a land he knows he never can. For the Christian this truth is but the necessary first act in a Divine Comedy. The history of the universe for the Christian is in principle already told. It is a delightful tale with but a spicing of momentary woe.[1]

I think that the *Reconquistas* would read those words and say, "No more hunkering down! Let us ride forth! Let us accept Christ's gracious offer to share in His victory!"

At this point, I hope that the reader might ask, "Who's right? Do we circle the wagons? Build the ark? Flee to the catacombs? Or do we ride forth?" I would say that

[1] Paul Weiss, *The God We Seek* (Carbondale: Southern Illinois Univ. Press, 1964), pp. 141–42.

this question, as stated, is incomplete. It must be complemented by further questions, such as, "Which strategy is right for me and the people in my care?" And that question must be made more specific by, "Which strategy is right for me and my dependents right now?"

Let us start with the first and simpler question: "Who's right?" My answer: "They all are." Faithful heirs and provident stewards of true Christendom must learn from all four strategies.

From those who would circle the wagons, Christians must learn the indispensable values of fellowship and teamwork. Christians may have to work in solitude, but they cannot afford isolation. Strays and stragglers are easily picked off.

From the ark-builders, Christians must learn the value of provident action and the dangers of procrastination. Ark-builders have overcome their "normalcy bias" and so are disinclined to dismiss or explain away warning signs both near and far.

From those denizens of the catacombs, Christians must learn shrewdness. Our Lord Himself urged His followers to become "wise as serpents and innocent as doves" (Mt 10:16). A lot of good work is done in the catacombs. A shrewd Christian will learn how to live both aboveground and underground.

From the *Reconquistas*, faithful Christians must learn to follow the good example of the "happy warrior" who, in the words of William Wordsworth:

> Finds comfort in himself and in his cause;
> And, while the mortal mist is gathering, draws
> His breath in confidence of Heaven's applause:
> This is the happy Warrior; this is he
> That every man in arms should wish to be.[2]

[2] William Wordsworth, "Character of the Happy Warrior".

The Christian happy warrior can show initiative when it is needed and leave the results to God.

Fighting a long war requires a stout heart and resilient morale. Saint Francis de Sales once quipped, *"Un saint triste est un triste saint."* (A sorrowing saint is a sorry saint.) The long war ahead of us must be fought by a band of such happy warriors and would likely be lost by sad and sorry saints.

Now to the harder questions: Which strategy is right for you and your dependents? Which strategy is right for you and your dependents in your own here-and-now? I do not know. How could I? I do not know you. I do not know your state in life, your health, your experience, your circumstances. Are you newly married? Are you pregnant? Are you a student? A soldier? A bishop? Are you a doctor in a Catholic hospital? A teacher in a public school? Do you live on a farm? Or in a city? Or in a cloister? Are you young or old? Wealthy or poor?

You and your dependents, individually and collectively, must study, pray, discern, and exercise the virtue of prudence. Remember that you must not do nothing; you must do something; and you cannot do everything. Also, make use of all the lessons offered by the four strategies described above.

In the next meditation, I will introduce some principles that can and should be used by all heirs and stewards of Christendom.

MEDITATION XLIII: Eight Principles

To help faithful Christians discern and act in light of the previous meditations, I will offer eight principles—three taken from a Catholic source and five taken from a secular source.

The Catholic source is the scholar and man of letters Joseph Pearce. He recently penned an essay entitled "The Three Pillars of the Resistance". Here I will summarize and adapt his three pillars for our purposes:

1. Be Christ-centered—we can only fail if we are not;
2. Be not anxious about the world's wickedness or anything beyond your immediate control;
3. Move from self-seeking to self-donation.

We can encapsulate these three principles for our purposes with the words of Saint John the Baptist: "He must increase, but I must decrease" (Jn 3:30).

The next five principles are quite freely translated from combat veteran Matt Graham's five rules for prevailing in life-or-death situations:

1. No passivity, procrastination, or excuses allowed—ever;
2. Everything truly important should be important to you;
3. Grace builds on nature—strive to give your best self to God's grace;
4. Do the hard things first;
5. Improvement begins by doing what needs to be done.

Christendom is a matter of life and death. Lives and souls are at stake. The holy must not be allowed to be vandalized. Who will defend the honor of the Virgin Bride of Christ who is the Church? The praiseworthy heirs and stewards of Christendom must never lose sight of these principles. Regardless of your circumstances, these eight principles can guide your discernment and action as you and yours seek answers to the questions of how to serve

Christendom. In the next meditation, I will ask perhaps the hardest question of all.

MEDITATION XLIV: The Hardest Question of All

"What time is it?"

Why is that such a difficult question? Because it can be so easy to accept as obvious and complete the many ways of answering that question. For example, could you say that any one of the following is the one, correct, final answer to the question, "What time is it?"

"It's 11:45 P.M."

"It's Thursday."

"It's the Thursday after Ash Wednesday."

"It's February."

"It's three weeks before my grandmother's birthday."

Would it help much if I added, "It's Year 'X' of the reign of this or that potentate or pope"?

Let us try to specify our discussion of time by asking, "What time is it for the Church?" By that I do not mean the chronological age of the Church. I mean, instead, in what era of the Church are we now living? A simple way of answering might be to say: "The Church is living in a post-Christian era and must recall and retrieve Christendom if she is to bring the world to a much-needed post post-Christian era."

Let us be a bit speculative and ask about what time it is in terms of the lifespan of the Church-on-earth, that is, the Church Militant. Many people try to glean an answer by scrying the Scriptures, the apparitions of Our Lady, or the pronouncements of popes or prophets. I can ask that question easily enough, but I dare not answer it.

Some people are sure that the Church Militant is entering "end times" or "the last days". Are we? I do not know. Our Lord said that no one knows the day or the hour but our Heavenly Father (Mt 24:36). I think that we should learn to live with that fact.

Nonetheless, Our Lord also commands us to "interpret the signs of the times" (Mt 16:3). This book is the product of reading the signs of the times, in light of and in service of Christendom, for all of my adult life. I can say with Christian confidence that this present post-Christian era cannot prevail and will not endure. I believe that the post post-Christian era that we can and should work to welcome and usher in can and should be a recalled and retrieved Christendom. Such a post post-Christian era will be good for man and for the greater glory of God.

The work of bringing forth that new era is above all the work of God, a work for which all Christians have been summoned and missioned. It can further humanize and divinize every aspect of human life—individual and communal, public and private, formal and informal.

In asking the question, "What time is it?" in relation to the era of the Church Militant and the service of Christendom, some further distinctions and clarifications are in order. We must address the issue of time as cyclical and as linear.

Simply put, it is easy to view time on earth as cyclical. Spring is followed by summer; summer is followed by autumn; autumn is followed by winter. The cycle repeats. We have come to call the phases of this cycle "seasons".

Likewise, the ancient tradition of the Church revolves in a cycle of liturgical seasons. Saints across the centuries have marked the cyclical revolving of liturgical time from Advent to Christmas to Lent to Easter to Pentecost, and so on.

So far, we have been speaking of time in near and familiar terms. Human reflection also speaks of time in abstract, cosmic, and absolute terms. Some pagan cultures viewed time as a whole as both cyclical and eternal. The motion from birth to death to birth is never-ending.

Some contemporary atheists see time as linear and without purpose or meaning. That is to say, time only starts, endures, and terminates. As Thomas Nagel describes it, "We are an episode between two oblivions." Said more eloquently by Shakespeare, the record of time is, "a tale told by an idiot, full of sound and fury, signifying nothing" (*Macbeth*, act 5, scene 5).

For linear time to be meaningful, for it to have a beginning, a middle, and an end, for it to result in success or failure rather than oblivion, it must unfold as a story guided by its author toward its fulfillment. To use the technical philosophical term, it must be teleological. God's goodness, wisdom, providence, and sovereignty demand that the passage of time be teleological, that it have within it an *entelechia*—that is, an impulse toward fulfillment, a drive toward the end for which it was made.

We are free to board the "Destiny Train" or to decline the invitation. But the train will leave the station and arrive at its destination with or without us.

The difficulty of speaking of time in terms of the era of the Church Militant is that the Church views time, both literally and metaphorically (as well as liturgically) as both cyclical and linear. As literally linear, the Church recognizes that we are living in the Year of Our Lord 2021, which was preceded by the year 2020. Whether any of us will make it to 2022 remains to be seen—except by God.

The Church's view of literal linear time is eschatological. That is, time will end, but reality will not. After time, eternity will remain. How each of us will spend eternity is of ultimate concern for all of us, whether we know it or not, whether we like it or not, whether we at this moment hope or despair or presume. In terms of literal cyclical time, the Church recognizes that it is now winter in the Northern Hemisphere and summer in the Southern Hemisphere.

In terms of liturgical time, the season of Lent has begun, based on a literal reckoning of the date of the first Sunday following the phase of the full moon nearest the Vernal Equinox.

What about time—as linear, as cyclical, as liturgical—taken metaphorically? Here I ask the reader to allow me some poetic license. I speak now in my own name only, simply offering my own considered opinion in response to the question, "What time is it?"

My answer: The Church Militant is inevitably tending toward consummation because God wills it. We are now living in a post-Christian era that I hope will be succeeded by a wiser and holier Christendom. Such a succession, I believe, will be good for man and pleasing to God.

To get from here to there, we must acknowledge where we are in the metaphorical cycle of seasons. Metaphorically speaking, we are in winter. How far we are into that season, how long it will last, how severe it will be—I do not know. But I cannot deny that it is winter—cold and death and hardness are all around us. Perhaps not within us, but surely around us.

We find ourselves now in the season of Lent, not just for forty days in the year 2021, but for years, perhaps decades—when that long Lent began, I cannot say with certainty; when that long Lent will end, I can only speculate, and I will not do so here.

Eschatologically, the Church Militant is nearer to the end, the fulfillment, than when she began. How much nearer, I do not know and will not here hazard a guess.

Are we living in a time of chastisement? Maybe. I can say more confidently that we are in a time of illumination. In very recent years in particular, "the thoughts out of many" are being revealed (Lk 2:35). During this time of illumination, I am confident that it will become more and more clear who our real friends and true enemies are.

In every sense, we are in Lent. As far as I can tell, we are at Gethsemane.

So—now what? What shall we heirs and stewards of Christendom do in these our times? It is winter; let us now prepare for spring planting. It is Lent; let us prepare for Easter.

ACKNOWLEDGMENTS

Here's a summary of several conversations I've had over the past year:

"You've written another book?"

"Yes."

"Don't you have anything else to do?"

"Well, yes—quite a lot actually, but this seemed important, so..."

"Is this one going to be like the last one you wrote?"

"Well, I certainly hope that I can attain again the heights of clarity, wit, and wisdom of..."

"No! I mean—is it going to be... you know..."

"Almost 300 pages and demanding the reader's uninterrupted attention?"

I will end the recollection here.

Perhaps it is peevish of me to recall more readily the struggles of writing than, with gratitude, the encouragement I have received from so many. My memory for names is imperfect, so the list of names that one expects in an acknowledgements page like this will be brief. To my dear friend of Brazilian origin, German temperament, and Jesuit spirit, I will say this much: "See—I really was paying attention during our years of conversation and correspondence. I hope this book proves that."

I would be remiss if I did not also say thank you to my family, who love me through all of my days; to the Society of Jesus, for granting me permission to publish this work; to my friends and colleagues at Ignatius Press who helped me to turn my scribbles into another book; and, in a special way, to the Faithful Remnant I have met, near and far, especially those committed to the First Saturdays.

Oremus pro invicem!